ECONOMIC ISSUES, PROBLEMS AND PERSPECTIVES

ECONOMICS OF COMPETITION

ECONOMIC ISSUES, PROBLEMS AND PERSPECTIVES

Additional books in this series can be found on Nova's website under the Series tab.

Additional e-books in this series can be found on Nova's website under the e-book tab.

GLOBAL ECONOMIC STUDIES

Additional books in this series can be found on Nova's website under the Series tab.

Additional e-books in this series can be found on Nova's website under the e-book tab.

ECONOMIC ISSUES, PROBLEMS AND PERSPECTIVES

ECONOMICS OF COMPETITION

GEORG LEISMULLER
AND
ELIAS J. SCHIMPF
EDITORS

nova publishers
New York

For permission to use material from this book please contact us:
Telephone 631-231-7269; Fax 631-231-8175
Web Site: http://www.novapublishers.com

NOTICE TO THE READER

Additional color graphics may be available in the e-book version of this book.

LIBRARY OF CONGRESS CATALOGING-IN-PUBLICATION DATA

Economics of competition / editors, Georg Leismuller and Elias J. Schimpf.
p. cm.
Includes index.
ISBN 978-1-62257-416-2 (hardcover)
1. Competition. 2. Antitrust law--Economic aspects. 3. Austrian school of economics. 4. Consumption (Economics) I. Leismuller, Georg. II. Schimpf, Elias J.
HD41.E33 2012 338.6'048--dc23 2012024281

Published by Nova Science Publishers, Inc. † New York

CONTENTS

PREFACE

According to conventional economic wisdom, it is believed that the beneficial functioning of competition is not secured spontaneously but must be supported by state action, i.e., specific antitrust laws and agencies. Hence, competition is regarded as an instance in which the visible hand of the state is believed to be needed in order to enable the invisible hand of the market to function more effectively. Topics discussed in this book include the competition and antitrust policy in the Austrian economic perspective; competition in the pharmaceutical market in Austria; a study of the greed factor in capitalism; consumption behaviors in a vertical differentiation model; the effects of mergers in the retail sector; and market competition with irrational agents.

Mainstream economics built upon neoclassical insights into the Pareto-efficiency qualities of perfectly competitive markets believe that the beneficial functioning of competition is not secured spontaneously but must be supported by state action. Economists from the Austrian School of Economics have been pioneering and trenchant in questioning this normative conclusion and even call for the repeal of antitrust policy. They maintain that standard microeconomics does not adequately account for the characteristic features of competition in the real world, and therefore advocates antitrust policy measures, which often has the effect to protect less efficient business organizations from competition rather than to promote free-market competition. Chapter 1 reviews the theoretical foundations underlying this view of the Austrian School of Economics on competition and antitrust policy. In particular, it shows (i) why the Austrian school questions the correctness of neoclassical theories on competition and views it instead as a dynamic, entrepreneurial discovery process, (ii) what requirements are crucial to unleash and maintain competition in this understanding, (iii) why given these requirements there is no pattern of action, which in and of itself is inconsistent with competition and (iv) why competition issues are best dealt within general economic policy.

As explained in Chapter 2, the Austrian market for self-medication is organised by way of a chain of monopolies. One of the world's strictest regulatory regimes to ensure that medicinal drugs are sold in pharmacies only, little in the way of competition between pharmacies, information asymmetries and full-scale regulation of prices and margins along the value-added chain have combined to create an inefficient market. With self-medication expected to gain ever more ground in Austria in the medium to long term, breaking up these market structures should produce high welfare gains for consumers through substantial price cuts. Negative effects of deregulation in terms of lower quality or less supply security, on the other hand, appear to be unlikely.

Chapter 3 posits that capitalism goes in two different directions: encouraging ambition or encouraging greed. The paper deals first with the orientations of the greedy versus the ambitious. Then it examines some key practices of the greedy and the ambitious. Finally, it emphasizes different orientations to curb greed and therefore support ambition.

In a vertically differentiated duopoly, Chapter 4 analyzes the firms' strategies when they face some consumption behaviors hardly studied in the literature. In a first essay, we consider conspicuous consumption, where the preferences of an individual depend positively on the quality consumed and negatively on the other good's quality in the market, accounting for relative preferences for quality. In the second essay, we deal with addictive ordinary goods in a dynamic setting where the perception of quality in the second period depends on the quality consumed at the first one.

According to EU competition law, mergers that significantly impedes effective competition, particularly by creating or strengthening a dominant position are prohibited. To identify these cases, authorities need a quantifiable model of the relationship between the variables that are affected by the merger and some measure of competition. Furthermore, the authorities must make their decision quickly, rendering deliberate data collection and econometric analyses infeasible in practice. The decision must be based on easily accessible data.

In Chapter 5, a simple model of the interaction between the retail and wholesale markets is constructed, calibrated and simulated based on a concrete case (the acquisition and merger of 250 shops previously organized in a voluntary chain of shops comprising roughly half of the market for high-end cosmetics in Denmark).

Model simulations predicts that the merger would most likely significantly affect retail prices. The harmful effects are markedly intensified through the possible abuse of buyer power to raise barriers to the market and curb the competitiveness of minor rivals. However, the dominant position is vulnerable if increased profits induce the entrance to the sector of more independent competitors. The competition authorities were justified in conditioning their approval on the removal of contract-based barriers to entry.

Analytically, the main results of this work are the following: (1) In a linear model characterized by heterogeneous products and constant marginal costs, the optimal (Nash equilibrium) wholesale price is unaffected by the structure in the retail sector. (2) The effect of buyer-power- induced quantity discounts depends crucially on the specific design of the rebate scheme: A relative discount on the list price that the independent shops are charged *increases* the average retail price, whereas a fixed reduction relative to the pre-merger price *reduces* the average retail price. (3) Buyer power-induced retail price maintenance (RPM) increases the average retail price. RPM increases the competitiveness and profits of the merged shops only if the producers keep the wholesale prices unchanged. If the producers adjust their wholesale prices, then RPM hurts both the merged and the independent shops and benefits only the producers. The harmful effects on consumer welfare and efficiency are intensified.

The equilibrium notions are derived based on the optimal behavior of rational agents. For example, the notion of perfect competition has been long established based on the presumption of firms maximizing their profits in the process of making their decisions with respect to whether they should enter a market, how much output to produce after they enter the market and when to exit the market. However, with irrational agents in the market instead of rational ones, where does the market competition take the market in the short run or long run? What types of agents would survive in the long run? Chapter 6 intends to review the research results in this part of the literature and point out the future research directions.

Chapter 7 examines how uncertainty about rival firm's behavior affects the equilibrium and its dynamics under heterogenous competition. A differentiated mixed duopoly is considered in which one firm sets a quantity and the other firm charges a price. It is demonstrated that behavioral uncertainty stabilizes the unstable dynamic process in comparison to behavioral certainty and generates Pareto-improvement in the sense that the firms can earn larger profits.

In: Economics of Competition
Editors: G. Leismuller and E. Schimpf
ISBN: 978-1-62257-416-2

Chapter 1

COMPETITION AND ANTITRUST POLICY: AN AUSTRIAN ECONOMICS PERSPECTIVE

"The advantages of competition do not depend on it being 'perfect'" (HAYEK, 1990, p. 65).

Jürgen Wandel*
Leibniz Institute of Agricultural Development in Central and Eastern Europe, Halle (Saale), Germany

Abstract

Mainstream economics built upon neoclassical insights into the Pareto-efficiency qualities of perfectly competitive markets believe that the beneficial functioning of competition is not secured spontaneously but must be supported by state action. Economists from the Austrian School of Economics have been pioneering and trenchant in questioning this normative conclusion and even call for the repeal of antitrust policy. They maintain that standard microeconomics does not adequately account for the characteristic features of competition in the real world, and therefore advocates antitrust policy measures, which often has the effect to protect less efficient business organizations from competition rather than to promote free-market competition. The article reviews the theoretical foundations underlying this view of the Austrian School of Economics on competition and antitrust policy. In particular, it shows (i) why the Austrian

* E-mail addresses: jwandel@gmx.de; wandel@iamo.de; Address: Leibniz Institute of Agricultural Development in Central and Eastern Euorpe, Halle (Saale), Germany.

school questions the correctness of neoclassical theories on competition and views it instead as a dynamic, entrepreneurial discovery process, (ii) what requirements are crucial to unleash and maintain competition in this understanding, (iii) why given these requirements there is no pattern of action, which in and of itself is inconsistent with competition and (iv) why competition issues are best dealt within general economic policy.

1. Introduction

According to conventional economic wisdom, it is believed that the beneficial functioning of competition is not secured spontaneously but must be supported by state action, i.e. specific antitrust laws and agencies. Hence, competition is regarded as an instance in which the visible hand of the state is believed to be needed in order to enable the invisible hand of the market to function more effectively. For most of the time standard neoclassical microeconomics built upon neoclassical insights into the Pareto-efficiency qualities of perfectly competitive equilibrium has been deployed to support this normative conclusion. All its variations (traditional price theory, structure-conduct-performance paradigm of industrial organization, game-theoretic oriented new empirical industrial organization) portray competition as an allocation mechanism leading to completely predictable outcomes in the form of a market equilibrium (Mantzavinos, 2006: 284). Accordingly, antitrust policy must take care that competition provides for the Paretian efficient use of production factors. Usually it is not based on a strict application of perfect competition but rather on the notion of “workable competition” as a second-best approximate to that ideal. Business practices that are alleged to prevent an optimal allocation of resources are then either prohibited per se (e.g. cartels) or prohibited or restricted on a rule of reason basis that weighs their potentials benefits against their potential costs (e.g. mergers).

In 2000, the European Union started to reform its competition policy towards a “more economic approach”, which implies an enhanced role of the rule of reason. It explicitly takes into account models of modern industrial organization theory which accepts that certain business practices associated with market power might promote economic efficiency. This necessitates a case-by-case assessment of the potential costs and benefits of an action deemed to be a threat to competition. It is claimed that, compared to a rule-oriented approach, the analytical and statistical tools of modern industrial economics are capable to allow competition policy to be more accurate in discriminating between business practices that promote economic efficiency and those that do not (Vanberg, 2009: 20).

Austrian economists have been pioneering and trenchant in questioning such a capability. In fact, many Austrians hold a special antitrust policy unnecessary and call for its repeal. It is maintained that the orthodox literature does not adequately account for the characteristic features of competition in the real world, and therefore leads to wrong normative conclusions for competition policy. All too often it in fact protects less efficient business organizations from competition rather than promotes free-market competition.

The article reviews the theoretical foundations underlying these conclusions on competition and antitrust policy of the Austrian School of Economics as typified by the works of Ludwig von Mises, Nobel Prize winner Friedrich A. von Hayek, Murray N. Rothbard and Israel M. Kirzner. The Austrian School is an approach to economics that originated in Vienna in the 1870s, with the publication of *Principles of Economics* by Carl Menger. With the threat of Nazism growing in Europe, the school's best known protagonists Mises and Hayek left Austria in the 1930s for the USA. As a result, the bulwark of the Austrian school today has shifted to the US universities, particularly New York, George Mason, and Auburn.

While in some ways consonant with the orthodox neoclassical and new institutional economics theorizing, the Austrian school holds a heterodox minority status, primarily in view of its rejection of mathematical modeling and statistical empirical methods. In spite of a wide range of views on certain issues, most Austrian school economists are united by their strict methodological individualism, subjectivism, a view of the market system as an incessant entrepreneurial discovery process, as well as strong doubts about the government's ability to intervene optimally into the economic system (Butler, 2010; Boettke 2010). Accordingly, the basic policy implication of the Austrian school is the uncompromising advocacy of free market policies. In the following the article will explain the theoretical reasoning underlying this implication with regard to competition issues. Section 2 will show why the Austrian school views competition differently than mainstream microeconomics, namely as a dynamic, entrepreneurial discovery process. Next, section 3 examines what requirements are held crucial to unleash and maintain competition in this understanding. Then section 4 explains why given these requirements there is no pattern of action, which in and of itself is inconsistent with competition and section 5 why competition issues are best dealt within general economic policy. Section 6 concludes the article.

2. The "Austrian" Understanding of Competition

2.1. Competition as Dynamic, Rivalrous Market Process

Austrian economists regard competition not as a state of affairs, which is called "competitive equilibrium" but as a dynamic process of interacting decisions of market participants in succeeding periods of time (Hayek, 1948: 96). It is a process, because not all decisions of the market participants may have led to the expected results, as the correspondent market participants might have been either too pessimistic or too optimistic. As a result, in the succeeding period of time, decisions will be revised. Competition is regarded as inherently rivalrous, because each market participant must not only pay careful heed to the prospective decisions of the actors on the other side of the market, but also to the prospective decisions of actual and potential competitors (Mises 1998: 274; Kirzner 1973: 12). If the economic agents fail to outdo their rivals they will suffer losses and might be driven out of the market.

From this dynamic and rivalrous view of competition follows that the so called "data" in the neoclassical model of perfect competition like qualities, prices, production technologies or preferences cannot be regarded as given. Rather, competition as a process involves a continuous change in exactly these data, brought about by the economic agents themselves (Kirzner 1997: 70). Therefore, competition can never be "perfect" and when these changes are assumed away "perfect" competition means "indeed the absence of all competitive activities" (Hayek 1948: 96).

2.2. The Knowledge Problem

Central to the Austrian understanding of the purpose of competition is the problem of knowledge. Hayek, the most eminent Austrian economist, has emphasized that the knowledge of human beings in and about complex phenomena like a modern market economy based on labour division is limited. This holds not only for the economic agents acting on the markets but also for the economist observing an economy. The reason for this are the limited cognitive abilities of every human being to capture and process all relevant information of place and time on which he bases his economic decisions. The most important information pertains to what's needed, who needs it, and who has the means to meet these needs.

Since this limitation is incurable, Hayek speaks of insuperable or "constitutional" limits to knowledge. In fact, the knowledge of relevant "circumstances of place and time" (Hayek, 1945: 524) is dispersed and fragmented among the many individuals who compose society, held separately and locally, and often contained in inarticulate forms. This tacit knowledge is often not consciously known even to those who possess it and it is more so never given to anyone in its totality, neither to any one of the economic subjects nor to observing scientists or any omniscient dictator (Hayek, 1945: 77f.). As a result it is held impossible to predict specific outcomes of the market process.[1]

The crucial question, which Hayek (1937 and 1945) considers to be the central economic problem, is then how society can make use of this dispersed knowledge "not given to anyone in its totality" (Hayek, 1945: 519) so that individuals can use it to achieve their ends mutually. Hence, in the Austrian view the economic problem of society is not a problem of how to allocate "given" resources. It is rather a problem of how to secure the best use of resources known to any of the members of society, for ends whose relative importance only those individuals know (ibd.). For this a mechanism is needed that activates and communicates information about which goods and services best satisfy the needs of the people.

2.3. Competition as a Discovery Procedure

According to Hayek (1945: 85f.) in market economies this information is codified in the changes in relative prices, which are generated and transmitted by market competition. For example, in the event of a natural disaster which has curtailed the availability of a specific raw material the fact of a reduced supply will be effectively communicated to potential users through the medium of a higher price – which also provides the incentive for the socially desirable economizing of the particular raw material (Hayek, 1945: 85f). Hence, it is the interactions of suppliers and demanders that generate market prices for various goods and services. These prices convey information about localized supply-and-demand conditions, indicating to suppliers where supplies are needed most and communicating to demanders when they may expand consumption (because supplies have become more abundant relative to

[1] This does not mean, that man is not able to make any predictions at all based on the knowledge he acquired through learning and past experience. However, this allows only for very general predictions of the *kind* of events which one must expect in a given situation, not of particular individual events. Hayek (1989: 4) calls this kind of predictions "pattern predictions".

demand) or curtail consumption (because supplies have become less abundant relative to demand) (Sobel and Leeson, 2008: 30).

Through its profit-and-loss mechanism competition provides the necessary incentive for individuals to acquire constantly for new knowledge, for example, about preferences, production technologies or appropriate organizational and institutional arrangements, and to use the information to meet their personal ends. If they do it successfully, they are rewarded by profits; otherwise they suffer losses which urge them to correct their errors. So, what competition does is the discovery of unsatisfied needs that no one had hitherto realized or at least used. This is why Hayek (1978: 253) called competition a "discovery procedure". If these needs and the means to meet them were already known or could be predicted, then competition would in fact be unnecessary. Just like in other events in life like sports, it would apparently "be absurd to arrange a competition if we knew in advance who the winner would be" (Hayek, 1978: 249). The discoveries are made through the experience the market participants by continually testing their plans in the market (Kirzner, 1973: 10). However, how any individual will act in detail and what particular circumstances he will encounter, is not known before even to him and must be still more unknown to anyone else (Hayek, 1990: 69).

It is this capacity to cope with the inescapable decentralization of knowledge to satisfy the individuals' needs of a society, in which Austrian economists see the key contribution of competition to social well-being. Competition is not needed to ensure a maximum of wealth in the sense of Pareto optimality, because this is in the constantly changing real world not achievable (Hayek, 1937). Surely, competition as a discovery procedure constantly reallocates resources over time so as to satisfy consumers as much as possible. So, in this sense it also contributes to an efficient allocation of resources and to a high level of social welfare because it will bring about a situation "where more of the potentially useful objective facts will be taken into account than would be done in any other procedure we know" (Hayek 1990: 68). However, Austrian economists neither claim that the allocation is "optimal" nor that it could be improved with government interventions.

2.4. The Entrepreneur as the Driving Force of Competition

Kirzner (1973, 1982, 1997) has emphasized, that the driving force in competition as a discovery procedure is the entrepreneur. That's why he (1982) calls competition an "entrepreneurial discovery process". The notion "entrepreneur" describes any alert economic agent, individuals as well large, complex business organizations. Alertness is understood as "noticing the potential for profitable venture" (Kirzner and Sautet, 2006: 22) or, put differently, as the discovery of gains from trade that were hitherto unknown to market participants (Sautet, 2010: 93). This "noticing" (discovery) may "consist of perceiving a price differential (arbitrage)... In most cases the alert "noticing" consists (in addition to becoming aware of relevant price differentials) of alertly noticing how physical resources can be assembled to generate (physically different) products – for example by the invention of a new technique, in an innovative, profitable manner" (Kirzner and Sautet, 2006: 3).

According to Kirzner (1973: 10ff.; 1982) and Sautet (2008) entrepreneurs are guided by *monetary profit*. The profit opportunities emerge and are discovered in a trial and error process. This is because individuals base their decisions on what they personally think are the best options available to them. These assessments are clearly likely to be in greater or lesser error.[2] Each of these mistaken decisions will systematically result in market losses, correct decisions in profits. As a result of these elementary profit or loss experiences, market participants are stimulated to less erroneous activity (Kirzner, 1982).[3]

What is important for normative conclusions is that entrepreneurial activity does not require perfect competition. On the contrary, in perfectly competitive markets there is neither scope nor any need for entrepreneurial initiative, because there is no uncertainty, so that "there is nothing left for the entrepreneur to do. He cannot find any opportunities to buy from sellers who underestimate the buying demand of their potential purchasers, in order to sell himself to these purchase-hungry buyers" (Kirzner 1973: 26f).

3. Crucial Requirements Crucial to Unleash and Maintain Competition as a Discovery Procedure

3.1. Institutional Conditions

The scope for entrepreneurial discoveries and the existence of economic agents with the ability and the desire to make and exploit discoveries are not sufficient

[2] Buyers may offer high prices because they erroneously believe that no one is able or prepared to sell for less. Sellers offer to sell at low prices because they think no one is prepared to buy for more.

[3] A seller who is disappointed in his expectation of securing a high price will learn that he can expect, at best, only a lower price. A seller who has accepted a price lower than the price being paid by buyers elsewhere in the market helps create a situation in which the same item is being traded at two different prices -- thus offering the opportunity to alert entrepreneurs to buy at the lower price and resell at the higher price. Such clearcut opportunities for pure profit tend to attract attention, to become exploited and thus eliminated -- in the course of which the initial error itself is likely to be corrected (Kirzner, 1982).

for the discovery process to take place. The economic agents must have the possibility to make and exploit them. This brings to bear the institutional conditions that are imperative to unleash and maintain competition as an entrepreneurial discovery process.

Kirzner (1982) argues that it is crucial that the economic agent have the freedom to act upon their discoveries, because the dynamic of competition comes from the implementation of entrepreneurial discoveries. Freedom to act includes therefore freedom to contract and "requires that no entrepreneur be blocked from entry into any line of market endeavor", i.e. freedom of entry. Freedom of entry is at the same time the most effective tool to protect competition as an entrepreneurial discovery process, because "so long as others are free to offer the most attractive opportunities they are aware of, no one is free from both the urge and the need to compete" (Kirzner 1973: 97f). Therefore, Kirzner (1973: 99; 1982; 1997: 74) considers freedom of entry the only crucial ("necessary and sufficient") institutional prerequisite to induce and maintain competition as a discovery procedure. In addition, clearly (formally or informally) defined and impartially enforceable individual property rights are necessary to *exploit* discovered profit opportunities (Kirzner 1973: 49; Kirzner and Sautet 2006: 18). Individual property rights give individuals the power to decide how to use and allocate resources, goods and services. If someone else holds these rights (e.g. an authoritarian government) or if they are attenuated or not enforced, the individual cannot, or only in a limited manner, trade with others. From this follows, that the quality of the institutional framework crucially determines the quality of competition as an entrepreneurial discovery process. As has also shown Mancur Olson (2000: 176ff) in order to *unfold the productive power* of competition as a discovery process t*o the fullest extent possible* well defined and secure property rights and an effective rule of law is necessary, because it increases transactional trust. Attenuation of property rights as well as various market regulations do not completely destroy the entrepreneurial discovery process but restrict it to self-enforcing trades on what he called "spontaneous" and "irrepressible" markets (bazaars, black markets, street hawkers) that do not provide for a high level of prosperity.

3.2. Barriers to Entry

Since freedom to entry is the crucial prerequisite to unleash and maintain competitions as an entrepreneurial discovery process it is important to clarify what Austrians exactly mean with this. For Austrian economists freedom to entry means exclusively the complete absence of legal or, as Kirzner (1982) also calls them, "extra-market" barriers to entry like import tariffs, subsidies, tax breaks, license requirements or other legal restrictions. They provide privileges to a few economic agents that enable them to charge a higher price than it would if they were competing directly with others in the market. Non-legal barriers to entry, that are usually set down as imperfectly competitive in textbooks of mainstream economists because they imply less than perfectly elastic demand curves facing firms, e.g. price discrimination, predatory pricing, advertising and other modes of product differentiation, tying agreements, refusal to supply or purchase or advantages due to size, are considered to be legitimate and appropriate "entrepreneurial" business practices in the competitive struggle to forestall entry of newcomers, since they make up the dynamic competitive process (Kirzner 1973: 170, 1997: 75).

All these non-legal barriers undeniably make it more difficult for newcomers to enter the market and constitute for them a *barrier*, but they can be overcome by superior performance and do in no way limit the *freedom* of entry. The freedom of entry would only be violated, if, for example in the case the entry into a market required from a newcomer a large amount of capital, he had raised the necessary capital and met all other requirements of being able to compete, such as having had assembled the necessary management and workers with the required skills, and then would have been forcibly prevented from entering the market by the government or other private economic subjects. The *freedom* to enter is, thus, not equal to the *ability* to enter an industry and therefore not the same as the barriers of entry of mainstream economics (Reisman 2002). For "Austrians" extra-market obstacles against entry constitute the only real harmful obstacles to competition as an entrepreneurial discovery process, because without them competition is, at least potentially, always present (Kirzner 1973: 98).

Besides government imposed barriers to entry, freedom to entry can also be harmed by private economic agents in ways that are illegitimate from an Austrian perspective. One way is to influence political decision-makers to get protection and the other to intimidate or extort competitors under the threat of force. In addition, Hayek (1990: 83ff; 2008: 230ff), but also Petro (2009) do not exclude that some non-violent business practices by powerful private economic agents might constitute harmful entry barriers, in particular price discriminations and boycotts against suppliers or buyers. For example, Hayek (1990: 84) holds price discrimination undesirable if it is used to coerce particular individuals or firms to deter or otherwise influence potential competitors. Yet, Hayek fails to explain (i) what the harmful effect of such a business policy for consumer well-being will be, (ii) how and under which conditions harmful coercion could be exercised and (iii) more importantly, how they can unequivocally be identified. Price discrimination can only be successfully carried out when a supplier is able to separate a market along different price elasticities of demand and to prevent arbitrage between the market segments. Both, the noticing of different price elasticities and the commercially successful use of this knowledge through setting different prices for different groups of consumers are nothing but entrepreneurial alertness. In the case that an incumbent offers favourable conditions only to customers in a certain region in order to keep newcomers out, these customers are nevertheless better served as before.

In spite of Hayek's less permissive view on discrimination practices most modern Austrian economists tend to hold only legal barriers to entry and the intimidation of competitors under the threat of force as violations of the freedom to entry and thus socially harmful. For deciding whether a business practice violates freedom to entry or not they suggest to check whether it violates someone else's property rights or not. Applied to boycotts Armentano (1999: 100f.) argues: "A consumer boycott of a manufacturer's product, for example, does not violate the property rights of the manufacturer; the manufacturer has no right to the consumer's income in the first place. Likewise, a restriction of production on the part of a manufacturer – a producer boycott – cannot violate the rights of consumers, since consumers, absent any contractual arrangement, have no property rights to the manifacturer's product".

4. Is Market Power a Problem in the Austrian Understanding of Competition?

These fundamentally different views on the nature and purpose of competition between neoclassical and Austrian economists lead to different implication on what is to be considered as market power. Principally, from an Austrian perspective there is no pattern of action and business structure, which in and of itself is inconsistent with competition, if there are no legal restrictions to the entry in markets and if property rights are secure. Then even the existence of one single supplier (monopoly) or a group of colluding firms (cartel) in a market is no economic problem, because the reason for the monopolistic position can only be superior skills (see also Kirzner 1973: 101ff.). In that case it would "be absurd to punish the possessor [of superior skills – added by the author] for doing better than anyone else by insisting that he should do as well as he can" (Hayek, 1990: 72). Open markets are enough to put a single producer under pressure to provide good products and services that meet consumer demands and ensure that market "power" is never permanent (Hayek 1990: 79). If under the conditions of complete freedom to entry monopolies nevertheless prevail for a long time, this only signals that other would-be producers are in fact not able to meet the demand at prices and qualities that this single producer does. Otherwise they would have entered the market.

Thus, certain market structures, forms of business organizations or the firm size are seen as the natural consequence of the competitive struggle and therefore not socially harmful. As Hayek (1990: 78) argues "the most effective size of the individual firm is as much one of the unknowns to be discovered by the market process as the prices, quantities or qualities of goods to be produced and sold". Moreover, it is maintained that "there can be no general rule about what is the desirable size since this will depend on the ever-changing technological and economic conditions; and there will always be many changes which will give advantage to enterprises of what on past standards will appear to be an excessive size" (Hayek, 1990: 77). In this context, it is not surprising that quantitative indicators of the status of competition like market shares, concentration ratios, the Lerner Index or price developments traditionally used in mainstream competition theory and politics are held flawed and useless for the following reasons: Measures of market concentration require an acceptable definition of "relevant market". However, determining the relevant market is an insurmountable problem (Armentano 1999: 83f), because it is far from evident what the nearest reasonable substitute for a certain product is. In fact, Austrian economists hold that "every commodity competes with all other commodities" (Mises 1998: 278), because producers are after the same thing, namely money (Krawisz 2010; Sautet 2007). Even if relevant markets could be clearly defined it is impossible to know which levels of market concentration generate market power. As Armentano (1999: 86) put it: "No one knows, or can know, whether monopoly power begins at a 36 percent market share or a 36.74-percent market share".

It is also difficult to relate unambiguously price and output developments to market power, because there are many other possible reasons for price and output changes, e.g. increases in demand or input prices, natural disasters or government interventions. Decomposition of these effects in empirical studies is difficult if not impossible.

Finally, the knowledge requirements to determine the deviation of the price from marginal cost as a measure of market power are underestimated. It is held impossible to objectively assess an individual's costs and to know what the competitive price is supposed to be (see also Shostak, 2000). Austrians contend that costs are *subjective* (Butler, 2010: 34). Although they can be dated at the moment an individual made his choice, they cannot be objectively evaluated, because this choice is based on anticipations about probable future developments and the perceptions of utility forgone at the moment of choice. Both the expectations of the producer and the utility forgone are individual and not objective, because the underlying preferences are subjective. Each person values forgone opportunities differently (Stringham, 2010: 46f.). In addition, Hayek (1990: 70) argues, that "the lowest costs at which a thing can be produced are exactly what we want competition to discover. They are not necessarily known to anyone but to him who has succeeded in discovering them."

Even given that costs could be objectively measured and be found out that a firm's prices are above marginal costs, there is again the problem to objectively and unambiguously relate this to market power, because there are many other possible reasons for a deviation of prices from marginal costs, e.g. increases in demand, or the adequate return on investment for an innovation. Once an entrepreneur introduces, for instance, a new product that appeals to consumers he inevitably acquires 100 % of the newly established market. It is, in fact, the profits from market power that are the engine that drives the economy. Therefore, unless it results from government protection, market power can never be harmful to competition and consumer welfare.

5. The Case Against Antitrust

The insurmountable knowledge problem that arises in the attempt to determine unambiguously market power and socially undesirable effects caused by it in an enormous complex and ever-changing market process and the resulting discretionary interventions is the major reason why Austrian economists reject real-world antitrust policy. For them any effort to assess and weigh potential costs and benefits of business practices in each single case is what Hayek (1989) called "pretence of knowledge." For example, in the case of an absolute per se prohibition of "collusions" (cartels) it is pretended that they only serve to restrict output – a social cost – but create little, if any, opportunity for the generation of social benefits since it doesn't involve an integration of facilities between firms. Yet, how can antitrust authorities and their economic advisors be sure that efficiencies and cost savings to society may not be associated with such agreements?[4] In the application of the rule-of-reason approach antitrust authorities

[4] Even given that such agreements may only restrict production and increase group profits, it is overlooked that they are generally not able to do so in the long-run in open markets, because high profit would attract newcomers. The general difficulty of cartels that usually prevents their longevity is to coordinate and police its own supply-restriction schemes, since participants are tempted to become free riders: Although they have an interest in others' respecting the

pretend to know the future course of the market process and how to distinguish unambiguously between good and bad market power. However, in the enormous complexity of socio-economic systems the capability to predict the overall, direct and indirect consequences that particular measures will produce in an intricate network of interdependent individual choices and in a dynamic process that is driven by the creativeness of adaptive human agents is severely limited.

In the attempt to account for this complexity modern industrial organization theory produced a multitude of highly refined models using game theory. However, often they are valid only under very specific assumptions and sometimes come to contradictory conclusions. Easterbrook (1984: 11) describes most accurately the situation as follows: "If we assembled twelve economists and gave them all the available data about a business practice, plus an unlimited computer budget, we would not get agreement about whether the practice promoted consumers' welfare or economic efficiency more broadly defined. They would discover some gaps in the data, some avenues requiring further exploration. Someone would invoke the principle of second best, claiming that monopoly could be a beneficial offset to distortions elsewhere. At least one of the economists would construct a new model showing how the practice *could re*duce efficiency if certain things (unknowable from the data) were present".

As a result the rule of reason approach leaves much room for arbitrary and discretionary decisions that leads to a situation where the antitrust agency "tells some businessmen that they must not cut prices, others that they must not raise prices, and still others that there is something evil in similar prices" (Hayek, 1990: 86). Such an approach means a loss in legal certainty because market participants can no longer tell from general rules of the game what strategies are prohibited, but that what they may do or not do depends on how the competition agencies, informed by their economic advisors, will assess the welfare consequences in particular instances (Vanberg, 2009: 21). As Armentano (1999) has found out in an analysis of the history of antitrust regulation, antitrust laws have often been employed against innovative business organizations that have expanded output and lowered prices to protect less efficient business organizations from competition rather than to promote the interests of consumers.

This leads to non-economic "Austrian" arguments against antitrust policy. Antitrust legislation is seen to harm due process and justice as well as the institution of private property and the freedom of action. It injures due process and justice, because often used notions like "reduce competition substantially",

agreement, they can expect a larger share of the common profit by introducing some degree of competition with regard to their partners (Armentano, 1999: 37).

"unreasonable" restraints of trade, "relevant market" or "price reduction to meet competition in good faith" lack any clarity and therefore make antitrust enforcement capricious and arbitrary (Armentano, 1999: 101). It violates private property rights because, as Hayek (1990: 72) explains: "The power to determine the price or the quality of a product at the figure most profitable … is a necessary consequence of the recognition of private property in particular things, and cannot be eliminated without abandoning the institution of private property. There is in this respect no difference between a manufacturer or merchant who built up a unique organization, or acquired a uniquely suitable site, and a painter who limits his output to what will bring him the largest income".

Similarly, Armentano (1999: 100) argues: "Private and peaceful activities such as price discrimination, merging, tying, and price fixing violate no property rights in the ordinary sense of the term; that is, they do not necessarily involve force, fraud, or misrepresentation. Yet, from a strictly natural-rights perspective, the antitrust laws themselves which regulate private and peaceful trade *are* inherently violative of property rights". Also collusion and output restriction are not held to violate the rights of potential buyers. "Producers own their property, or are the trustees of property for owners, and possess all the rights to it, including the absolute right not to use it at all. Similarly, consumers have full rights to their own property, including the absolute right to spend or not spend their own money. The individual rights (property rights) of neither party can be violated by a refusal to deal or by a partial refusal to deal through, say, some voluntary restraint of trade" (ibd.).

Concerning the freedom of action Hayek (1990: 72f.) makes clear: "So long as any producer is in a monopoly position because he can produce at costs lower than anybody else can, and sells at prices which are lower than those which anybody else can sell, that is all we can hope to achieve – even though we can in theory conceive of a better use of resources which, however, we have no way of realizing…Not to do as well as one could, cannot be treated as an offence in a free society in which each is allowed to choose the manner of employing his person and property…We know how to induce such individuals or organizations to serve their fellows better than anyone else can do. But we have no means of always making them serve the public as well as they could".

Austrian economists maintain that competition as an entrepreneurial discovery process is protected best within the framework of general economic policy. Since the absence of legal restrictions to entry in markets is the crucial prerequisite to unleash and maintain competition, the main task of the economic policy is seen in keeping markets open, accompanied by setting up and protecting a functioning institutional framework that channels entrepreneurial activity in socially beneficial directions. Hayek developed three requirements that these institutions (rules) must meet: (1) They shall be abstract in the sense that they merely describe those actions which are not allowed and leave it to the individuals to discover innovative modes of action (Hayek, 2008: 183). (2) They must be general, i.e. applicable to unknown and indefinite number of persons and cases (Hayek, 1973: 73). (3) They must be certain, i.e. valid for a long time, so that the economic agents can build stable expectations (Hayek, 1973: 270f.). Moreover, government policy must refrain from any regulations that negatively affect financials gains as the crucial motivation of the entrepreneur, e.g. a heavy tax burden, price or profit controls (Kirzner and Sautet 2006: 14ff.).

While there is not much disagreement on the primary importance of these institutional requirements to maintain competition views nevertheless differ within the Austrian school as to the need for extra regulation for some business practices alleged to menace freedom to action. The most prominent advocate for a, however, very limited scope of antitrust measure is Hayek. As has been shown in the section on barriers to entry, he does not rule out that price discrimination might be used to coerce a certain market conduct upon individual or firms and suggests making it the basis for a claim of damage. Likewise, he pledges that agreements on cartels and collusion shall be declared invalid from the very beginning and unenforceable in court (Hayek 1990: 86). This suggestion is not equal to a call for a general prohibition of voluntary agreements. Hayek (ibd.) in fact opposes this because "there is much reason to believe that some wholly voluntary organizations of firms that do not rely on compulsion are not only not harmful but actually beneficial. It would seem that prohibition under penalties cannot be carried out without a discretionary power of granting exemptions, or by imposing upon courts the difficult task of deciding whether a particular agreement is, or is not, in the public interest."

Conclusion

The article highlighted an alternative, largely ignored theoretical perspective on the understanding of competition and its normative implication for competition policy. Antitrust policy in real world market economies, like the EU's more economic approach, rests largely on an understanding of competition put forward by standard microeconomic theory as a static state of affairs and a mechanism of optimal resource allocation. Business practices are then assessed if and to what extent they improve economic efficiency, often in a case-by-case manner.

Austrian economists flatly reject such a view and provide strong arguments why we can have faith in the self-healing power of the market process and why therefore special antitrust regulations are not only superfluous but generate malign consequences. They emphasize that competition is a rivalrous entrepreneurial process by which the knowledge enabling a better coordination of individual plans is discovered over time. For this competitive process to take place and bring socially desirable results a set of institutions are necessary that guarantee the functioning of entrepreneurial discovery and the exploitation of business opportunities over time. These institutions must guarantee entry into any market to anyone desiring to compete.

Real-world antitrust laws largely underestimate the complexity of the market process socio-economic systems and human agents' limited cognitive abilities that severely limit the capability of regulators to predict the overall welfare consequences of certain business practices. The discretionary interference with the entrepreneurial discovery process resulting from a case-by-case assessment not only increases legal uncertainty, but all too often protects some producers from the greater efficiency of their potential competitors under the disguise of consumer protection. Thus, it inhibits the discovery of consumer preferences and the flow of resources from less efficient suppliers to more efficient suppliers. Consequently, the cure it prescribes is worse than the disease. Therefore, antitrust policy should be repealed.

References

Armentano, D.T. (1999). *Antitrust. The Case for Repeal*, revised 2nd ed. Auburn, Alabama: The Ludwig von Mises Institute.

Boettke, P.J. (ed., 2010): *Handbook on Contemporary Austrian Economics*. Cheltkam, Uk, Northampton, MA, USA: Edward Elgar.

Bulter, E. (2010): *Austrian Economics. A Primer.* Adam Smith Institute: Adam Smith Research Trust 2010 *(http://www.adamsmith.org/sites/default/files/resources/austrian-primer-text.pdf)*.

Easterbrook, F.H. (1984): The Limits of Antitrust. *Texas Law Review*, 63 (1), 1 – 40.

Hayek, F.A. (1937): Economics and Knowledge. *Economica,* 4, 33 -54.

Hayek, F.A. (1945). The Use of Knowledge in Society. In F.A. Hayek (1980), *Individualism and Economic Order* (pp. 77-91). Chicago, London: University of Chicago Press.

Hayek, F.A. (1973). *Law, Legislation and Liberty, Vol.1: Rules and Order.* Chicago: University of Chicago Press.

Hayek, F.A. (1976). *Law, Legislation and Liberty, Vol.2: The Mirage of Social Justice.* Chicago: University of Chicago Press

Hayek, F.A. (1978). Competition as a Discovery Procedure. In F. A. Hayek (Ed.), *New Studies in Philosophy, Politics, and Economics and the History of Ideas* (pp. 179–90). Chicago: University of Chicago Press.

Hayek, F.A. (1989). The Pretence of Knowledge. *American Economic Review*, 79 (6), 3-7.

Hayek, F.A. (1990). *Law, Legislation and Liberty, Vol.3: The Political Order of a Free People*. Chicago: University of Chicago Press.

Hayek, F.A. (2008): *The Constitution of Liberty*, Reprint. London, New York: Routledge.

Kirzner, I.M. (1973). *Competition and Entrepreneurship*. Chicago: The University Chicago Press.

Kirzner, I.M. (1982). Competition, Regulation, and the Market Process: An "Austrian" Perspective. *Cato Policy Analysis No. 18. www.cato.org/pub_display.php?pub_id=884*. Accessed 26 November 2009.

Kirzner, I.M (1997): Entrepreneurial Discovery and the Competitive Market Process: An Austrian Approach, *Journal of Economic Literature*, Vol. 35, No. 1 (March), pp. 60-85,

Kirzner, I.M. and Sautet, F. (2006). *The Nature and Role of Entrepreneurship in Markets: Implications for Policy.* Mercatus Policy Series. Policy Primer No. 4, June. Mercatus Center, George Mason University.

Krawisz, D. (2010). The Meaning of Competition. *Mises Daily*: April 13, 2010. *http://mises.org/daily/4233/The-Meaning-of-Competition*. Accessed 7 February 2011.

Mantzavinos, C. (2006): The institutional-evolutionary antitrust model. *European Journal of Law and Economics*, 22 (3), 273-291.

Mises, L. (1998). *Human action. A Treatise on Economics*. The Scholar's Edition. The Ludwig von Mises Institute, Auburn, Alabama.

Olson, M. (2000). *Power and Prosperity: Outgrowing Communist and Capitalist Dictatorships*. Oxford University Press.

Petro, S. (2009). Do Antritrust Laws Preserve Competition? *Mises Daily*, 24 November 2009; http://mises.org/daily/3856, first printed in *The Freeman*, 1958. Accessed 28 January 2010.

Reisman, G. (2002): Understanding Barriers to Entry. *The Free Market*, 20 (1). *http://mises.org/freemarket_detail.aspx?control=384*. Accessed 15 December 2009.

Sautet, F.E. (2007). The shaky foundations of competition law. *New Zealand Law Journal,* June, 186-190.

Sautet, F.E. (2008): Ventures in Rebuilding: The Role of Entrepreneurship in the Post-Disaster Context, *Local Knowledge*, No. 1, Summer, Mercatus Center, *http://mercatus.org/sites/default/files/6_fredsautet.pdf.* Accessed 14 January 2012.

Sautet, F. E. (2010). The competitive market is a process of entrepreneurial discovery. In P.J. Boettke (Ed.), *Handbook on Contemporary Austrian Economics*, Cheltham, UK, Northampton, MA, USA: Edward Edgar Publishing, pp. 87 – 108.

Shostak, F. (2000): Judge Jackson's Bad Economics, *Ludwig von Mises Institute, Daliy Articles, June 8. http://www.mises.org/fullstory.aspx?Id=441.* Accessed 14 April 2005.

Sobel, R. and Leeson, P. (2008): The Use of Knowledge in Natural Disaster Relief management. *Local Knowledge*, No. 1, Summer, *http://mercatus.org/sites/default/files/8_sobelleeson.pdf.* Accessed 14 January 2012.

Stringham, E.P (2010): Economic value and cost are subjective. In P.J. Boettke (Ed.), *Handbook on Contemporary Austrian Economics*, Cheltham, UK, Northampton, MA, USA: Edward Edgar Publishing, 43 – 66.

Vanberg, V.J. (2009): *Consumer Welfare, Total Welfare and Economic Freedom –On the Normative Foundations of Competition Policy*. Freiburg Discussion Papers on Constitutional Economics 09/3. Walter Eucken Institut, Freiburg.

In: Economics of Competition
Editors: G. Leismuller and E. Schimpf
ISBN: 978-1-62257-416-2

Chapter 2

THE MARKET FOR SELF-MEDICATION IN AUSTRIA: THE COMPETITION ECONOMIST'S POINT OF VIEW

Michael H. Boeheim[1,*] and Eva Pichler[2]
[1]Austrian Institute for Economic Research, Austria
[2]Institute for Economic Policy and Industrial Economics, Vienna University of Economics and Business, Austria

Abstract

The Austrian market for self-medication is organised by way of a chain of monopolies. One of the world's strictest regulatory regimes to ensure that medicinal drugs are sold in pharmacies only, little in the way of competition between pharmacies, information asymmetries and full-scale regulation of prices and margins along the value-added chain have combined to create an inefficient market. With self-medication expected to gain ever more ground in Austria in the medium to long term, breaking up these market structures should produce high welfare gains for consumers through substantial price cuts. Negative effects of deregulation in terms of lower quality or less supply security, on the other hand, appear to be unlikely.

---

* E-mail address: michael.boeheim@wifo.ac.at. (Corresponding author)

A. Introduction

In the field of pharmaceutical products, the market segment of non-prescription drugs is known as self-medication or over-the-counter (OTC) market. In Austria, this segment is subject to distribution restrictions by way of a rule ("Apothekenpflicht") that the sale of medicinal products is permitted only in *Apotheken* (pharmacies, i.e. dedicated shops that are alone entitled to dispense medicinal products and are run by a university-graduated apothecary). Compared to other countries the OTC market is minute in Austria, even though Austrian spending on health care by far exceeds average levels[1]. The OTC segment operates in the shadow of a refunding market[2] and – as its smaller sibling – is subject to strict regulations: the fact that medicinal products may be sold only in pharmacies combines with the world's strictest prescription-only regime and regulated prices and margins in logistics and distribution (mostly through pharmacies) to ensure that competition is dampened, prices remain high and the market's volume and growth potential are inhibited. Even generics have trouble penetrating into this sheltered market segment.

Yet there are quite a few factors that point at the growing importance of this market in the medium to long term: for one, the demographic change in the age pyramid will raise demand for pharmaceuticals in general while, secondly, health awareness is on the rise in the population. The definition of "healthy" is getting ever more exacting, new diseases are "discovered" all the time, and there are fluid boundaries to the booming wellness market. The trend could be further enhanced by future reforms of the health care system that involve cuts in benefits paid by the health insurance institutes for "minor" ailments (such as the common cold). And last but not least, Austrian health care consumers (who, labelled as "patients", have been used to being assigned a solely passive role in the public discussion) may well attain a higher level of information and elect to use self-medication more often – because information becomes more easily accessible on the internet and is thus more intensely used. Considering such factors, it appears desirable to improve the market's performance.

In some indication sectors and in spite of the large number of companies in the OTC market, producer concentration appears to be considerable (same as in the refunding market) and rising further, due to a wave of mergers. Added to this is that consumers typically are faced with an information gap: although the

[1] Cf. OECD, OECD Health Data (Paris, 2008).

[2] The refunding market comprises all prescription medicines (both those that require a head physician's approval and those freely prescribed by the physician) the cost of which are paid (refunded) by the health insurance funds.

European Court of Justice has recently set aside the advertising ban, comparing product prices is still difficult for consumers. As pharmacies do not have the spatial capacity enabling them to present their entire range of products, consumers need to explicitly ask for alternative products, and pharmacists will not be interested in offering them the cheapest alternatives first. Consequently, original drugs have no need to fear competition from generics. What's more, generics producers have few incentives to offer prices substantially below those for original products, as competition does not work along the price criterion. As a result, prices vary little between products – a sign not so much of intense competition but rather of its failure. In keen contrast to the market for state-refunded medicinal drugs, where the Federation of Austrian Social Insurance Institutions forces generics and original drugs to fight it out over prices, they appear to come to a quieter and more profitable arrangement on the OTC market. Market performance – especially in terms of price and diversity – thus needs to be judged as unsatisfactory.

Overall, the impression prevails that, on the one hand, producers enjoy considerable market power in setting their prices, and, on the other hand, highly excessive margins are ubiquitous when it comes to product distribution through pharmacies, as margins in the OTC sector are designed to be generous and unresponsive to incentives.[3] Accordingly, pricing in the OTC market is the result of a *two-stage chain of monopolies* – a market form that economists agree is particularly inefficient and has an especially negative impact on welfare.[4]

Added to this is the fact that few groups in Austria actually have a stake in liberalisation: the Chamber of Pharmacists is its natural opponent, the Chamber of Physicians is sceptical about according patients responsibility (and especially the right to self-medication) as this could reduce patient turnover. OTC producers benefit more from smaller quantities at higher prices than from large quantities at lower prices, and, as they frequently supply refunded products as well, they have little interest in campaigning for liberalisation in the self-medication market, since they collaborate with wholesalers and pharmacies also in other – and much larger – segments. Wholesalers cannot be expected to fight for liberalisation, as they fear that it would lead to products being supplied directly from the producers to the retail (chainstore) chemists, thus circumventing the wholesale margin. Even the Health Ministry dithers, minding that any wrong OTC treatment might lead to high follow-up costs for the public health care system. The Federation of Austrian

---

[3] Only wholesale trading in OTC products is subject to the same margins that apply for the refunding market.

[4] See generally D.W. Carlton and J.M. Perloff, Modern Industrial Organization (Boston, Pearson, 4th edn, 2005).

Social Insurance Institutions, which rigorously controls prices in the refunding market, abstains from the OTC market as it does not pay for such products. Chemists, being potential beneficiaries of liberalisation, do not even try to fight against this array of interest groups, as expected profits are not worth the costs. Even the European Commission has so far been unable to achieve a political consensus on liberalising the OTC market.

B. The Austrian OTC Market

1. Market Definition

The OTC market is defined as comprising medicinal products (whether registered or not) for which no prescription is necessary but which may be sold in a pharmacy only. Dietary supplements and cosmetic products claiming to have a health-promoting effect are not included in this definition.

Table 1. Size of the self-medication market in Austria

	2007 (€ million)	Percentage change against previous year 2006-07	Proportion (%)
Pharmacy market, total	3,995.30	6.7	100.0
OTC market	482.20	5.8	12.1

Source: IGEPHA, Jahresbericht Austrian Self-Medication Industry (Vienna, 2008).

Table 2. Segments of the OTC market in Austria

	2007 (€ million)	Percentage change against previous year 2006-07	Proportion (%)
Pharmacy market, total	3,995.30	6.7	100.0
OTC market	482.20	5.8	100.0
Prescribed OTC medicinal products	39.20	1.7	8.1
Self-medication, registered OTC products	299.80	4.3	62.2
Self-medication, non-registered OTC products	143.20	10.3	29.7

Source: IGEPHA, Jahresbericht Austrian Self-Medication Industry (Vienna, 2008).

At almost € 500 million, total OTC sales make up some 12 % of the overall pharmaceutical market in Austria (Table 1). Of this, 91 % are products purchased for self-medication, two thirds of which are registered medicinal products (Table 2).

Medicine against cough and cold, vitamins and minerals, painkillers and anti-rheumatic pills are the chief market segments for self-medication. Together the three groups constitute just over half the OTC segment (Table 3).

Table 3. Markets for self-medication 2007

Pharmacy sales price	**2007 (€ million)**	**Percentage change against previous year *2006/07***	**Proportion (%)**
Self-medication market, total	443.00	6.2	100.0
Medicine against cough and cold	103.00	13.0	23.3
Vitamins/minerals	69.60	1.2	15.7
Painkillers and anti-rheumatic agents	54.10	6.8	12.2
Skin and mucus agents	41.90	2.1	9.5
Medicine for the stomach and digestion	41.00	7.5	9.3
Tonics/geriatrics	27.40	0.2	6.2
Cardiac stimulants	24.10	2.4	5.4
Medicine for bladder and reproductive organs	23.50	-0.7	5.3
Ophthalmic agents	16.10	11.6	3.6
Sedatives/sleeping pills	14.10	10.9	3.2

Source: IGEPHA, Jahresbericht Austrian Self-Medication Industry (Vienna, 2008).

Compared to other countries, people in Austria spend relatively little on self-medication (Table 4).

At 7.5 %, Austria ranks in the lowest third, topping only Greece, Slovenia, France and Spain in its spending on self-medication. Compared to Germany and Switzerland, Austrian consumers appear to be reluctant to choose self-medication even though health is considered a "luxury" and Austria ranks higher in terms of income. The EU average is higher than the Austrian rate by more than half. These findings change little even when, alternatively, we use absolute figures for OTC spending.

The market's dynamism is similarly unimpressive: During 2000-07, the OTC market in general managed a nominal rate of growth of 2.2 %, in real terms almost equivalent to stagnation[5] – a glaring difference to the refunding market[6] which is characterised by brisk growth that, at least in the view of the Federation of Austrian Social Insurance Institutions, is difficult to control. This paper, however, will concentrate on the OTC market.

Table 4. European self-medication market 2005-07

	Price ex works (€ million)			Proportion (%) of overall pharma market
	2005	**2006**	**2007**	**2007**
Austria	290	285	300	7.5
Belgium	595	619	634	15.1
Croatia	143	153	165	10.9
Czech Republic	376	375	485	25.8
Denmark	212	222	241	8.9
Finland	275	242	273	10.9
France	1,697	1,846	1,926	6.2
Germany	4,749	4,530	4,497	12.3
Greece	350	364	435	7.4
Hungary	284	301	287	13.9
Ireland	248	274	315	15.2
Italy	1,639	1,523	1,588	8.3
Netherlands	568	597	628	11.2
Norway	205	239	253	12.0
Poland	1,309	1,427	1,663	26.4
Portugal	238	284	267	7.5
Romania	166	364	458	23.2
Russia	2,130	2,690	3,050	24.5
Slovakia	124	147	168	13.7
Slovenia	31	32	33	6.7
Spain	600	595	618	4.4
Sweden	326	348	367	9.2
Switzerland	594	584	566	16.3
United Kingdom	3,033	3,191	3,385	12.7
EU-25	**17,111**	**17,565**	**18,567**	10.7
Europe	**20,183**	**21,230**	**22,601**	11.6

Source: AESGP (Association of the European Self-Medication Industry), *European Self-Medication Industry. AESGP Figures & Facts (*Bruxelles, 2008).

[5] Authors' calculations according to data from IGEPHA, Jahresbericht Austrian Self-Medication Industry (Vienna, 2008).

[6] Pharmig, Daten und Fakten (Vienna, 2008).

The Austrian association of the self-medication industry IGEPHA comprises 59 ordinary members who operate in the Austrian OTC market. Of these the most well-known are (in alphabetical order) Bayer, Böhringer Ingelheim, Croma Pharma, Drapal, Herba Chemosan, Johnson & Johnson, Kwizda Pharma, M.C.M. Klosterfrau, Novartis, Procter & Gamble, Ratiopharm, Sandoz, Sanofi Aventis and Sanova. After acquiring Metochem Pharma GmbH, Kwizda GmbH advanced to become Austria's number one OTC supplier with total group sales of about € 700 million and domestic sales (refunding market and OTC market) of about € 50 million. The Kwizda group is a major operator in wholesaling medicinal products and has recently amassed stakes in a large number of pharmacies, consequently holding a major market position throughout the pharmaceutical value-added chain (production – wholesale – retail).

Empirical evidence indicates that – same as in the refunding market – in spite of the relatively large number of suppliers to the self-medication market, market concentration is high in the various therapeutical categories as companies specialise in certain lucrative market segments. Comparatively few substitutes are available within product groups, and generics appear to be in a weak position: original drugs such as Aspirin, Supradyn, Tomaphyrin or Leaton retain their market lead in spite of being substantially more expensive than generics from equivalent active components. At present, many Austrian companies have managed to build up a strong presence in the OTC market, with the major pharmaceuticals acting as added players. Thus Meda Pharma Austria, a "minor" player, has achieved a 60 % share in the magnesium market and ranks an honourable second in the calcium market.[7] In the long term, the market is expected to further concentrate through mergers: local suppliers lacking a presence in international markets will be gobbled up by multinationals and their independent brands will disappear from the market.[8]

C. Regulation of the OTC Market

The Austrian self-medication market is among the most strictly regulated markets world-wide: all pharmaceuticals approved by the Federal Ministry of Health, regardless of whether they are registered or not, may, without exception, be sold solely in pharmacies. This distributive restriction is further bolstered by the world's strictest prescription scheme (source: information obtained from the price

[7] See www.welldone.at, issue of 30 December 2006.

[8] For a detailled discussion see F. Santermans, Herausforderungen für die Europäische OTC-Industrie: Chancen und Risiken, (Bonn, DUV, 2004).

commission at the Austrian Health Ministry). As a consequence, the OTC market is intentionally kept small compared to other countries.

Dietary supplements and cosmetic products with "health promoting features" do not count as OTC products and their sale is not restricted to pharmacies. Nevertheless, there have over the past decades been repeated instances where chemists lost to pharmacies the right to sell products listed as dietary supplements. The use of medicinal arguments to boost sales is a prevailing practice in this field.

Product pricing is fully regulated throughout the entire value-added chain, from the producer's price ex works to the pharmacist's purchase price to the price at which the product is sold to the customer: producers are required to *orient* themselves at the European average price (EU-15) because too high a mark-up results in an official enquiry (a tool which is rarely applied). Once a product is on the market, lack of competitive pressure ensures that its price will stay up. In the refunding market, on the other hand, product prices will decline over their life-cycle[9] because a constant stream of new products – whether generics or original drugs of similar or better properties – enters the market, which causes the Federation of Austrian Social Insurance Institutions to cut refunding prices. Declining prices are a typical feature of a product that originally achieves a high R&D mark-up but where the value of the innovation declines over time.[10] In the OTC market, however, this mechanism is made ineffective by regulation, to the detriment of consumers.

Wholesalers are obliged to distribute OTC products at the same terms as products for the refunding market (which are similarly regulated). This is the only stage where the OTC market does not suffer a disadvantage over the refunding market.

Pharmacies, however, are granted the explicit right to apply *significantly* higher mark-ups to OTC products than to refunded products. The latter are regulated on the basis of the pharmacy's purchase price (Table 5). The intermediate price thus computed is further increased by another mark-up of 15 %. On average, the pharmacy mark-up constitutes 60.8 % of the price on delivery (= price ex works plus wholesale margin).[11]

With the majority of OTC products purchased by the pharmacy at less than € 20, the pharmacies thus add an estimated *average mark-up* on OTC products of at least 55 %.

---

[9] See Pharmig, supra n 6.

[10] See W.S. Comanor, "The political economy of the pharmaceutical industry, (1986) Journal of Economic Literature Vol. 24/3, 1178-1217.

[11] See FOPI, Analyse der Abschätzung von Optimierungspotentialen im Arzneimittelbereich (Vienna, 2008).

Table 5. Regulated mark-ups by pharmacies in the refunding market

Pharmacy's purchase prise from	Pharmacy's purchase price to	Mark-up	Purchase price
0.00	10.00	39.00%	
10.01	10.22		13.90
10.23	20.00	36.00%	
20.01	20.45		27.20
20.46	30.00	33.00%	
30.01	30.93		39.90
30.94	60.00	29.00%	
60.01	62.42		77.40
62.43	100.00	24.00%	
100.01	104.20		124.00
104.21	120.00	19.00%	
120.01	124.17		142.80
124.18	150.00	15.00%	
150.01	156.82		172.50
156.83	200.00	10.00%	
200.01	207.55		220.00
207.56	350.00	6.00%	
350.01	357.07		371.00
357.08		3.90%	

Source: Österreichische Apothekenzeitung 2003, vol. 24.

For their OTC products, pharmacies incur higher inventory carrying costs (at least in terms of quantities) because these products enjoy less customer loyalty (compared to prescriptions which are refunded by the state). Nevertheless it can be assumed that the rate of turnover even for OTC products is substantially higher than that incurred by other businesses, as evidenced by the fact that wholesalers make delivery runs at least twice a day (!) at constant prices. Accordingly, inventory carrying costs are reduced to an absolute minimum. Combined with the monopoly on dispensing medicinal drugs, this regulation provides for a significant economic rent that is not passed on to customers.

Quite apart from the excessive margins (which do not reflect the underlying risk) a fundamental issue is how to justify restricting to pharmacies the right to sell medicinal products. To the extent that pharmacies combine their sale of products with advisory services, the pharmacist does have a special role. Whether this justifies the general restriction (which could be reasoned as a market failure) must be doubted. For one, recent tests by the consumer advocacy group *Verein fuer Konsumenteninformation*[12] confirm that advisory services delivered by pharmacies do not always achieve the high quality level constantly argued by their Chamber; and secondly, the need to give advice on self-medication drugs, which is anyway significantly reduced compared to that for prescription drugs, could be provided for through obligatory staff training in other distribution channels.

D. Price Formation by a Chain of Monopolies

When a consumer purchases a medicinal product from the OTC market, it can be assumed from the underlying market structure that its producer chooses a price near the monopoly price after which the pharmacy (in its capacity of monopoly distributor) adds another monopoly-type mark-up.

This price formation quite corresponds to the kind of pricing found in a chain of vertically linked monopolies. Such a "price design" was first described by *David Ricardo* as "double marginalisation".[13] The double mark-up is found in goods which are produced and distributed in a multi-stage process that would, e.g., involve extracting raw materials, processing them and selling the final product. Where the different stages are undertaken by different companies and where these enjoy market power (e.g. in the form of a monopoly), a new mark-up is added at each new stage. As a consequence of this double marginalisation, the final product is higher-priced than it would be if a single company controlled the entire production process. In the self-medication market, price policy thus works as follows: as the (downstream) monopolist nearer to the consumer, the pharmacy selects the monopoly price, given the producer's purchase price. In this way, the marginal revenue function of the downstream monopolist (i.e. the pharmacy) becomes the demand function of the upstream monopolist (i.e. the pharmaceutical producer). Each then chooses its product price by equating the marginal revenue function from its demand function to its marginal costs. The result is a double monopoly mark-up ("double marginalisation"), and a price that by far exceeds the classical monopoly price. A chain of monopolies thus leads to prices that are even higher than the monopoly price of a vertically integrated company. Consumers have to make do with a low economic rent, and the cumulated profits achieved by companies are lower than monopoly profits.

[12] See VKI, „Beratung in Tiroler Apotheken: Grassierender Beratungsnotstand“ (2008), Konsument 11.

[13] See D.W. Carlton and J.M. Perloff, supra n 4, Ch. 12.

Such an inefficient market structure provides an incentive for monopolists to attempt vertical integration which allows them to achieve the "classical" monopoly prices at lower mark-ups and thus generate higher profits. For consumers, the gain of this structure is in an improvement in market performance.

On the OTC market, vertical integration can be achieved only to a limited extent since products must be sold in pharmacies. At best, producers can acquire a stake in pharmacies, a practice which is on the rise in Austria (e.g. Kwizda GmbH) and is expected to proliferate further. Efforts to increase vertical integration can be found in cross-border internet sales (which the European Court of Justice has allowed for OTC products as well). If OTC products were permitted to be sold by chainstore chemists, house brands (which are sold at a much cheaper price) could be expected to strongly increase their presence.

E. International Practices to Regulate the OTC Market

Many European countries have liberalised their OTC sector and allowed some exceptions to the prescription-only regime. Italy, Hungary, Croatia and the United Kingdom permit non-prescription medicines to be sold by other businesses. In Germany, efforts are under way to evade the high margins – even in the refunding market. Consumers can hand over their prescription to a "Pharma Punkt" at a chemist's which passes it on to a pharmacy domiciled in the Netherlands. Consumers then pick up their order or have it delivered by mail, and pay by remittance. The service also includes OTC products which can be bought at a lower price.

Two rulings by the European Court of Justice have intervened in this market: one lifted the advertising ban for OTC products, the other permitted internet pharmacies to supply their products across borders to other EU member states. Already, internet selling appears to have penetrated some segments.[14] In Austria this has created the absurd situation that domestic pharmacies are not allowed to sell over the internet while their Common Market competitors are free and increasingly eager to export to Austria.

The European Commission has so far shied away from the pivotal decision – full liberalisation of the OTC market. A complex web of contrasting interests, nourished by the issue's proximity to the public health system, is expected to prevent any coordinated approach in the foreseeable future.

[14] Arbeiterkammer Wien, Medikamente aus dem Netz (Vienna, 2007).

Experience in the Netherlands has shown that liberalising the sale of pharmaceuticals, when accompanied by proper regulation and supervision, has produced only benefits for consumers. The knee-jerk "argument" furnished by the Austrian lobby (Chamber of Pharmacists), which, without bothering about empirical evidence, automatically assumes that liberalisation will translate into lower quality for consumers[15] is nothing more than a defensive rearguard action in the face of such empirical facts.

The Netherlands liberalised the market already in 1999. At the time, the country's established pharmacies feared competition from the chainstores. Groups such as OPG and German wholesalers such as Celesio and Phoenix were raring to conquer half the market at least. Yet their expansion drive has so far proceeded at a sluggish pace only: ten years after liberalisation, just a third of the almost 1,900 Dutch pharmacies are in the hands of chains.

The reason: the old-established pharmacies suddenly set out to court their patients and to improve the quality of their service. As a matter of course, Dutch pharmacies now make free deliveries to customers and have improved their advisory services. The fact that Dutch pharmacies have managed to retain the loyalty of their customer stock even after liberalisation goes to show that a focus on innovation and customer satisfaction will allow pharmacies to survive in liberalised markets. Yet the former monopoly rents were thoroughly skimmed: Before liberalisation, a pharmacy managed to turn an average profit of € 200,000 to 250,000; afterwards that figure had gone down to € 100,000.[16] The skimming of "pharmacy rents" has benefited customers through lower prices at a quality that has, at least, remained unchanged. Considering the similarity of the situation in Austria, liberalisation in this country could well produce savings for the public health system and for consumers of similarly substantial dimensions.

F. Consumer Information

While price comparison is easy for most products needed on a daily basis, the same does not apply to non-prescription medicines. Most pharmacies have no section that is freely accessible to consumers and where it would be possible to display product prices (perhaps even standardised to customary unit sizes).

[15] A recent study by the consumer advocacy group VKI (2008) showed that even the sheltered Austrian system is not able to automatically ensure maximum advisory quality. Sample tests of pharmacies in Tyrol found deficiences of an occasionally serious scope. Advisory services were described as being friendly but frequently incompetent. Some of the tested pharmacies were found to take the prescription-only regime too lightly.

[16] See J. Hoffritz, „Die große Verkettung“ (2008), Die Zeit, Nr. 51.

Customers need to explicitly enquire for alternative or cheaper products, and pharmacists have few incentives to show them low-margin products as this would cut down on their profit. In such a market getting price information is notoriously difficult. Accordingly, most consumers are inadequately informed about the relative prices of competing products. This information deficit is well-known to pharmaceutical companies and they exploit it to their advantage by keeping down price variations for comparable products. In other words: there is no competition on price in the OTC market.

Industrial economic literature demonstrates that in a monopolistic market already a low level of incomplete consumer information suffices to produce monopoly prices.[17]

In addition to the vertical market structures described, this appears to contribute substantially to a further weakening of competitive pressure and to companies being able to make the most of their monopoly situation. Considering that in this sector consumer demand is typically inelastic,[18] lack of information is a crucial factor in keeping prices high.

A simple and effective method to stimulate competition at little cost and with the added bonus of retaining grown structures would be to extend the *price marking obligation* to pharmacies: similar products would have to be listed for easy comparison, and basic medical information should be accessible (e.g. through a touchscreen operated by consumers in the pharmacy). Such a measure would strengthen the incentive for generics to enter the market and would provide an incentive to become competitive by undercutting prices and leave the high price level currently chosen by all suppliers.

G. Market Performance - Summary Evaluation

To summarise: several factors point at a finding that OTC market performance is driven by prices that are excessive due to the prevailing regulatory regime:

- High concentration of suppliers in the therapy categories.
- EU average price is used for orientation only when prices are first set; any decline in this price is ignored.

---

[17] See P. Diamond, P., "A model of price adjustment" (1971), Journal of Economic Theory 3, 881-894 and D.W. Carlton and J.M. Perloff, supra n 4, Ch. 13.

[18] For an overview see F. Breyer , P. Zweifel and P. Kiffman, Gesundheitsökonomie (Berlin, Springer, 2003) and R.E. Santerre, R.E. and S.P. Neuen, Health Economics: Theories, insights, and industry studies (Chicago, Irwin, 2006), Ch. 3..

- In contrast to the refunding market, an OTC product, once launched, is not exposed to competitive pressure which would make it cheaper over its life cycle due to the appearance of new competitive products.
- Most consumers are insufficiently informed because pharmacies have little incentive to provide information.
- With consumers suffering from an information deficit, price elasticity of demand is low in most therapy categories.
- Sales margins are regulated: particularly notable is the high margin in the OTC market which appears to be more than 55 % in spite of a high rate of inventory turnover and a constant stream of deliveries from wholesalers.
- Consequent to the strong market position enjoyed by producers *and* pharmacists, the price derives from a *chain of monopolies* and is markedly above the classical monopoly price.
- The strategy chosen by Austria to reduce VAT by 50 % is less than adequate because if combats a symptom rather than the cause of the high prices, which is in the market structure.

The benefit of an overall regulatory regime is that tax cuts for existing products are mostly passed on to consumers, because producers cannot quickly adjust the prices of their products without the approval of the regulatory authority and because margins are also regulated for the downstream sectors. Yet for new products, the reduced VAT rate could lead to a higher launching price, and in this way a large part of the tax cut would, in the long term, be "redistributed" to the market suppliers.

On the other hand, consistent and overall deregulation would achieve a *multiple* of the current tax relief effect for consumers without causing the revenue authorities to lose an estimated € 40 million in tax receipts per year.[19]

[19] See M. Boeheim, „Zur Rolle der Wettbewerbspolitik in der Inflationsbekämpfung“ (2008) WIFO-Monatsberichte 9, 693-706 and Wettbewerbskommission, Gutachten der Wettbewerbskommission vom 14.7.2008 gemäß § 16 Abs. 1 Wettbewerbsgesetz an den Bundesminister für Wirtschaft und Arbeit (Vienna, 2008).

In: Economics of Competition
Editors: G. Leismuller and E. Schimpf
ISBN: 978-1-62257-416-2

Chapter 3

THE GREED FACTOR: THE INSIDIOUS ENEMY THAT IS BEING IGNORED

A. Coskun Samli[*]
Marketing and International Business, Coggin College of Business, University of North Florida, Jacksonville, FL, US

Abstract

This article posits that capitalism goes in two different directions: encouraging ambition or encouraging greed. The paper deals first with the orientations of the greedy versus the ambitious. Then it examines some key practices of the greedy and the ambitious. Finally, it emphasizes different orientations to curb greed and therefore support ambition.

Introduction

When Schumpeter called innovation as "creative destructionist" certainly he did not mean to support the recent concept of "vulture capitalism" which creates unemployment at the advancement of making much money. Ratigan (2012) discuss them as corporate vampires. Vampire industries and vampire companies prey on their customers… "they don't make money they just take it" (p8). After

[*] E-mail address: jsamli@unf.edu. For Correspondence: Coggin College of Business, University of North Florida, Jacksonville, FL 32224.

all capitalism is not just making money for a few privileged people or organizations it is advancing a society and making it more prosperous for all.

At the writing of this paper millions of Americans are complaining that ninety-nine percent of the society is working for one percent. Indeed between 1979 and 2007 the earnings of the upper one percent has increased by 275 percent the income of the middle income group of 60 percent increased by only 40 percent and the income of the lowest fifth of our society increased only by 18 percent (CBO 2011).

This situation is described as the financial crises in the American economy. Hansen and Movahedi (2010) explain the current financial situation that created the deepest recession of recent history, which started a housing bubble which became extremely dangerous. It almost sent the American financial sector into total bankruptcy and created a very wide spread unemployment picture. Perhaps in order to understand this complex and extremely alarming situation, it may be important to make a distinction between individual motivational issues and organizational structures (Marx 1967). However, in our advanced industrial society these two layers of behaviors are becoming co-mingled with a very negative pattern for the industrial foundations of our society. Unfortunately, a very small group of multimillionaires have become extremely powerful and controlling the society in such a way that their economic well-being is constantly improving as more and more Americans are becoming poor.

From Ambition to Greed

Ideally capitalism "allows individuals to choose how they allocate their time where (and if) they work and what to do with their money they earn" (Hicks 2004). These were very important motivations for individual entrepreneurs at the earlier stages of modern American capitalism. Ambitious and entrepreneurial people developed the industrial fabric of our country. They were hardworking and ambitious and they created employment and economic wealth. Unfortunately, as small firms became industrial giants the individuals who are at the top of these industrial giants became greedy rather than being ambitious. Their egotistic pursuits of self-interest created insatiable passions and appetites for more financial power (Hansen and Movahedi 2010, Durkheim 1951). Marx coined this behavior as "boundless greed after riches (Marx 1967). Whereas Rand and Boesky maintained greed is good, (Hicks 2004, Boesky 1986) they did not distinguish between ambition and greed. Samli (2010) stated that the 21st century capitalism with its freewheeling, no enforcement of any authority, tremendously powerful self-interest and lacking consideration for the society as a whole, is gaining much power at the expense of the workers, the poor and the elderly. Certain select CEOs and corporate entities are behaving as if the society's economic well-being is a zero-sum game which means that blind selfishness will emasculate the possibilities of a fair and widespread economic growth (Wachtel 2003).

> "Whereas the ambition factor is reasonably constructive and rewarding both to the individual and the society, the greed factor, although possibly very lucrative to the individual, can be and in most cases is extremely destructive to the society. It is even more so globally, since stakes are greater and controls are even weaker (Samli 2010, 10).

In order to check the greed factor it is necessary to understand its orientation and its practices.

A Comparative Analysis

Understanding greed factor is articulated by contrasting it with ambition factor. Exhibit 1 puts forth such an effort. The two concepts are analyzed and contrasted on the basis of six key points of analysis these are constructive atmosphere perception of the world, personality traits, time dimension, civic-mindedness and selfishness element.

The greed factor displays itself in the form of a "get them before they get you mentality." It drives individuals to win in any way shape or form. It brings about the feeling that people's advancement depends on just how many people they can walk over. The ambition factor on the other hand, generates the feeling that working and collaborating with other people enhances opportunities for progress. In other words it enhances entrepreneurial orientation. Here the understanding is that there is room for advancement not only for one person at the expense of all others, but there is room for progress and opportunity for all.

In terms of the perception of the world the greed factor moves in the direction of getting everything one can possibly get. The world is there and getting anything basically means taking things away from others. Since the world is developed, our advancement will be based on others' loss.

The ambition factor, on the other hand, generates the feeling that working and collaborating with other people enhances opportunities for progress on a large scale basis. Here the understanding is that there is room for advancement not only for one person or for select few at the expense of the society, but there is room for progress and opportunity for all.

From the perception of the world point of view, the greed factor moves in the direction of getting everything one can possibly get. Since the world is already developed, getting things basically means taking things away from others. In a developed world advancement is based on others' loss.

The ambition factor, on the other hand, advocates that there is much progress that can be made and that progress can be very good for all participants. The world can be changed and improved. All people can benefit from such change and improvement. In terms of personality traits of those that are under the spell of the greed factor are that they are selfish and quite mean. They think in terms of "I am going to get mine whatever it takes and nobody should stand in my way." Again, people who are motivated by the ambition factor have different personality traits. They are generous, knowledge sharing and forward looking about existing and potential opportunities. They work cooperatively with others and let others also advance as they advance themselves.

Time dimension for the greed factor followers is now. They want everything and they want it now. There is no time to waste and, therefore, it should not be wasted. Ambitious people, on the other hand, realize that there is time for improvement. In fact, good performance and advancement take time. We can wait they think as long as there is progress. There is enough time for everything. Civic mindedness of the greed factor group is not really paying any attention to the environment. They see environmental efforts as costly and unnecessary. Their general orientation is "I don't care about pollution, nor do I care about the poor or the elderly. I must make as much money as possible. The ambitious group takes the position that if the environment is improved and if the poor and elderly are cared for there will be more money and, as a result, more jobs and more benefits for everyone. The poor and the elderly will buy my products or services which will further stimulate the whole economy.

The greedy will express selfishness by saying that "I must get all what I can for number one (me) and this should not have any limits and barriers." This is basically their goal. Whatever happens to other people is not a problem for the greedy. The ambitious element, however, considers the fact that there is much talent out there and that the whole society will benefit from the utilization of this talent. Progress is teamwork and working with others is synergistic (Samli 2010).

Although Exhibit 1 illustrates two extreme pictures of greed and ambition, it must be recognized that at one point there may be only a fine line between the two. It is certainly reasonable to believe that all human beings can be ambitious but this ambition could easily turn into an extreme level of greed. This point indicates that there is a necessity of having ambition checked and the greed possibilities need to be blocked. If ambition reaches a point of great success it could easily turn into greed. As once it was stated brilliantly, power corrupts, and absolute power corrupts absolutely. When Bill Gates developed the preliminaries of windows in a dorm room, it was ambition. However, subsequently some courts both in the U.S. and in Europe claimed the fact that Microsoft started using its power in an abusive manner and have been exercising a stifling monopoly over competition and competitors. The ambition has become greed. The greedy and the ambitious have quit different modus operandi.

Differences in the Practices

Exhibit 2 illustrates the critical contradictions between the practices of the greedy and the practices of the ambitious. As can be seen, the ambition factor can be very constructive for the future and progress, the greed factor creates a larger gap between haves and have-nots.

The greedy try to minimize or eliminate competition by mergers or acquisitions, the ambitious increase competition and employment by expansion. From this perspective it may easily be said that greed is the enemy of ambition. Ambitious and successful newly emerging small businesses are being gobbled up by greedy corporate pirates.

The greedy limit the pay of subordinates, thinking that there will be more remaining for them. The ambitious, on the other hand, hope to generate a better distribution of income so that the markets will also be greater and that would be beneficial to the society. The greedy will outsource only to lower costs so that there will be more profit for them. The ambitious will outsource to improve quality and to create more participation of others so that there will be a more even distribution of benefits for all and therefore create a consumer surplus.

The greedy will use their economic powers to receive unfair and excessive favors from the existing political establishments at the loss of the whole society. The ambitious will be engaged in spreading the power base as much as possible so that equal opportunity for the poor and under privileged will be expanded so that the society could advance.

The greedy will not share the profits with those who help them to generate those profits. The ambitious will consider the contribution of the entire participant in the economic activity in proportion to their participation and their contribution. This will create even greater profits in the future to be shared equitably. At this point it becomes obvious that the society will go backwards if the greedy can get their way. During the past decade or so the extra ordinary efforts in the U.S. to privatize and deregulate has already caused a tremendous discrepancy between the economic well-being of the top one percent of the income category and the rest of the society. This is a dangerous trend. According to some mass media reporting about seven of the richest people of the country have greater economic well-being than about ninety eight millionAmericans. This could get even worse if some corrective action does not take place.

Destructive Practices of the Greedy

Exhibit 3 illustrates some of the most destructive practices of the greedy. Although the practices listed are well known and do not need to be discuss individually the following needs to be emphasized. Laying off workers in recessions has become almost a common practice of global giants. They try to maintain their profit levels by cutting labor costs rather than, perhaps, accelerating their proactive marketing activities. They are what Ratigan (2012) calls capitalist who take rather than capitalism types of business that are sucking-up the blood of our industrial system.

Perhaps part of the major destructive activity is being engaged in union busting. If the thinking is that the size of the pizza is fixed than trying to get a larger slice of it would be not paying as much to labor. How do you accomplish that? Of course by union busting. Again, if it is assumed that the size of pizza, or profit picture, is limited, eliminating possible competition became a major activity. This is performed by merger mania which has been going on in our society since about the beginning 1980s (Samli 2001).

The same argument goes for radical innovations created by disruptive technologies. The alternative energy explorations have been blocked by the petroleum lobby in our society. There is no doubt that availability of money, rather than the well-being and the future of our society is controlling national economic decisions approved or encouraged by the U.S. Congress. As Ratigan (2012) posits the greedy are making fortunes by skimming money from the customers. This has been going on for a long while now. Dual pay check families are not a concept indicating ambition but are a response of the consumers to the squeezing forces exerted by the greedy. This is the result of reduced salaries imposed upon the workers in our society about since early 1980s.

Key Practices of the Ambitious

Exhibit 4 deals with this all important topic. Above all ambitious are the capitalists who make as opposed to those who take (Ratigan 2012). They are typically supporters of major innovations and they create jobs. Not only do they hire more people, they also work very closely with them and give them credit for what they do. The ambitious works with labor groups and recognize the importance of labor in their progress. Rewarding work is one of the most important features of this group. They share the proceed of the total activity. As mentioned earlier they do not lay off people instead bear the burden of a recession equally by taking cuts in salaries if necessary. Finally, this group is not attached to existing technologies. They look for new ideas and new ways therefore they support disruptive technologies and radical innovations (Samli 2008).

Combatting Greed

Without harming individual freedoms and positive economic initiatives, it is extremely critical that the greed factor must be checked. There are at least three general areas that need to be considered in counteracting greed, ethical, legal, and financial.

Ethical Counter Greed

Perhaps this movement started earlier than the other two. This idea may be supported by the increasing courses in the business curricula during the past decade or so. It is only hoped that these courses are primarily supporting ambition and condemning greed, but it is not quite definite that this is what is happening. But by definition, these courses can make a strong case for ambition which certainly is critically needed in our society. It is necessary for business ethics courses to consider the greed versus ambition issues with the hopes that articulating ambition for the common good will overpowers the greed.

Legal Counter Greed

Any attempt to create monopoly power or reduce competition must be outlawed. Although this sentiment has been articulated by antitrust laws it certainly has not been enforced forcefully. Since early 1980s this country has been plagued by merger mania which, by definition, creates monopoly power or reduces competition in the market. This pattern has not stopped and many major industries have become one step closer to an oligopoly. In addition limiting competition oligopolies create tremendous discrepancies in income distribution. This point was implied by J. K.

Galbraith as early as 1956, subsequently many authors reasserted the same point (Samli 2001). Invariably, oligopolistic tendencies lead in the direction of the greed factor. Leaders of oligopolistic firms become extremely rich and powerful and, as stated above, rather ruthless and greedy. In some extreme cases such as displayed by Enron a company that put individuals at risk for health related illness and death by instigating illegal and unfair manipulation of electric power in California (Hansen and Movahedi 2010). Perhaps, much of the discussions of white collar crimes are results of the greed factor which resulted due to lack of legal constraints. If the greed factor is allowed to proceed unchecked the government sooner or later will be forced to regulate and even over regulate (Barton 2011). However, the greed factor, at the writing of this article, needs to be regulated so that the American capitalism will have a future.

Financial Counter Greed

Greed basically receives its power and is based on financial resources and financial gains. Obviously, if it were decided that greed needs to be somewhat curbed, it will have to be curbed primarily financially. This financial curbing may have at least three prongs to consider: income, capital, sharing of resources. Here income includes resources that are used to meet immediate needs. Capital is unused income converted into different types of stockpiling that generates further market power (Hill and Cassill 2004). The sharing of resources is the third prong of the financial control considerations, it is considered to be an investment of group capital to enhance individual survival in the community or the society (Hill and Cassill 2004). It is obvious that each of these three prongs need to be studied and dealt with in detail one at a time and then all three considered together. Suffice it to say here that through regulations and taxation laws the acquisition and distribution of income, capital and resources need to be arranged so that the ambition factor will be supported and the greed factor is closely controlled.

Conclusion

This paper deals with perhaps one of the most critical and misunderstood social issues that is a great danger to our society. It must be understood that left alone ambition could become greed and the benefits of ambition that moves a society into a progressive state could dissipate and the society could become regressive. Although some thinkers propose that in time natural selection would shape the rules both greed and sharing into certain patterns of behavior (Hill and Cassill 2004). If such behaviors operationalize the corporations' mission values goals and objectives would operationalize the acquisition and distribution of income and resources. In the 21st century super dynamic societal and managerial conditions may either take a dangerously longtime to make conditions beneficial for all or those conditions which may not materialize. Because of these questionable outcomes a proactive thinking and coping with the greed factor are necessary.

Exhibit 1. Contrasting Greed and Ambition

Greed Factor		Ambition Factor
	Constructive Atmosphere	
Get them before they get you. Win anyway can step on many bodies as needed.		Working and collaborating with people. There are opportunities for everyone
	Perception of the World	
Get as much as you can at any cost. You cannot change the world. Exploit it.		There could be much progress through cooperation and mutual advancement
	Personality Traits	
Mean, grabbing, I got mine you do whatever you do as long as you don't stand in my way orientation		Generous, sharing knowledge and opportunity. Working with others and allowing others to raise themselves way of orientation.
	Time Dimension	
What do I want? Everything. When do I want them now? There is no time		There is time for improvement and advancement. We can wait as long as there is progress.
	Civic Mindedness	
I don't care about the environment. I don't care about the poor. My well-being is critical.		If the environment is improved, if the poor have more money we will be better off.
	Selfishness Element	
Must get all that I can for the number one (me). There should not be any limits.		There is enough talent for progress. If the society was better we all benefit.

Source: Adapted and revised from Samli (2010).

Exhibit 2. Differences in the Practices of the Greedy Versus Ambitious

Practices of the Greedy	Practices of the Ambitious
Likes to expand by buying out competition or competition reducing mergers	Likes to expand by starting by new plants as creates more employment
Blocks increases in minimum wages. Gives unrealistic raises to those who are very rich and powerful	Supports better distribution of income and progress for all
Outsources not to improve quality but to maximize profits that go to the top management	Outsources to improve quality and participation of others
Uses its power to receive greater favors from the political bodies	Emphasizes spreading the power base to as many as possible
Does not share proceed with those contribute much to the profitability	Shares proceeds with all others as proportionately as possible.

Source: Adapted and revised from Samli 2010.

Exhibit 3. Some of the Key Destructive Practices of the Greedy

• Laying off workers in recessions to maintain profits
• Venture capitalism, buying out companies that are struggling and putting them out of existence for large returns
• Union busting to take away bargaining positions of labor
• Exercising merger mania to limit competition
• Blocking off developments of disruptive technologies
• Influencing politicians to maintain low tax rates
• Charging exorbitant penalties for delayed loan payments
• Reducing salaries and requiring more work of labor

Exhibit 4. Some of the Key Constructive Practices of the Ambitious

• Starting new businesses and creating jobs
• Being partially or fully responsible for innovations
• Hiring more people and working closely with them
• Giving credit for the work associates do
• Working closely with the unions or labor groups
• Rewarding work equitable associates perform
• In recessions do not lay off people they bear the burden equitably
• Support disruptive technologies as much as possible

References

Barton, Dominic (2011), "Capitalism for the Long Term," *Harvard Business Review*, March, 85-91.

Congressional Budget Office (2011), *"Trends in the Distribution of Household Income Between* 1979 and 2007", Washington D.C., October, X.

Durkheim, Emile (1951), *Suicide*, New York: Free Press.

Galbraith, John Kenneth (1956), *American Capitalism*, Boston: Houghton Mifflin Co.

Hansen, Laura L., and Movahedi, SiaMak (2010), *Sociological Forum*, June, 367-374.

Hicks, Douglas A. (2004), *"Taming the Best: Virtues of Corporate Life"*.

Hill, Ronald Paul and Cassill, Deby Lee (2004), The Nat urological View of the Corporation and Its Social Responsibility: An Extension of the Frederick Model of Corporation Community Relationships," *Business and Society Review*, 3, 281-296.

Marx, Karl (1967), *Capital*, Vol. 1, New York: International Publishers.

Ratigan, Dylan (2012), *Greedy Bastards*, N. Y.: Simon Schuster.

Samli, A. Coskun (2010), *Globalization From the Bottom Up*, New York: Springer.

Samli, A. Coskun (2001), *Empowering The American Consumer*, Westport, Connecticut: Quorum Books.

Samli, A. Coskun (2008), *International Entrepreneurship*, New York: Springer.

Schumpeter, Joseph (1934), *The Theory of Economic Development*, Cambridge: Harvard University Press.

Wachtel, Paul (2003), "Full Pockets Empty Lives: A Psychoanalytic Exploration of the Contemporary Culture of Greed," *The American Journal of Pschoanalysis*, June, 203-233.

In: Economics of Competition
Editors: G. Leismuller and E. Schimpf
ISBN: 978-1-62257-416-2

Chapter 4

ESSAYS ON CONSUMPTION BEHAVIORS IN A VERTICAL DIFFERENTIATION MODEL

***Nada Ben Elhadj*[1,*], *Amal Hili*[2,†] *and Rim Lahmandi-Ayed*[3,‡]**
[1]LIM-EPT, Université de Carthage and ISG, Université de Tunis, Tunis
[2]LIM-EPT, Université de Carthage, FDSEPS,
Université de Sousse and GREQAM, Université de la Méditerranée, France
[3]LIM-EPT and ESSAI, Université de Carthage, France

Abstract

In a vertically differentiated duopoly, we analyze the firms' strategies when they face some consumption behaviors hardly studied in the literature. In a first essay, we consider conspicuous consumption, where the preferences of an individual depend positively on the quality consumed and negatively on the other good's quality in the market, accounting for relative preferences for quality. In the second essay, we deal with addictive ordinary goods in a dynamic setting where the perception of quality in the second period depends on the quality consumed at the first one.

JEL Classification: L11, L13, D43, C73

Keywords: Vertical Differentiation, relative preferences, quality choice, habit formation, dynamic model, addictive good

---

*E-mail address: nadabelhadj@yahoo.com
†E-mail address: hili_amal@yahoo.fr
‡E-mail address: rim_lahmandi@yahoo.com

1. Introduction

Vertical Product Differentiation models account for some markets where consumers agree on the ranking of variants, but differ by the willingness to pay for quality. The pioneering work on Vertical Product Differentiation is the model of Mussa and Rosen (1978), followed by Gabszewicz and Thisse (1979), Shaked and Sutton (1982, 1983) and Tirole (1988).

Several topics of interest have been investigated through vertical product differentiation models such as entry deterrence strategies and the finiteness property (Dixit, 1979; Shaked and Sutton, 1982, 1983; Lahmandi-Ayed, 2000; etc.). Some other works characterized the quality choice of firms without ex-ante hypothesis on the full coverage of the market and show accordingly that the consumers' demand are endogenous outcomes of firms' strategic interactions (Wauthy, 1996; Alvisi, 2000). In addition, several studies on vertical differentiation dedicated to the analysis of network externalities where the demand for a product is positively or negatively affected by the number of buyers (de Palma and Leruth, 1989; Reitman, 1991; Bental and Spiegel, 1995; etc.) and products' compatibility issues (Jeanneret and Verdier, 1996; Baake and Boom, 2001; Ghazzai and Lahmandi-Ayed, 2009; etc.).

Apart the analysis of the network externalities, too little attention has been paid to the impact of specific consumers' behaviors on vertically differentiated markets such as the consumption of organic products, the imitation behavior among consumers or the consumption of conspicuous and addictive goods, etc. In this work, we investigate these two latter effects of consumption behaviors through two variants of the Mussa and Rosen's model of Vertical Product Differentiation.

In the first essay, we assume that consumers exhibit relative preferences for product quality which we define as the consumer's satisfaction derived from having the best product in terms of quality compared with the other products present in the market. Conversely, the fact of having a product of lower quality causes a loss in the consumer's utility. The assumption that utility, status or happiness depend at least in part on the comparison of one's own consumption and good's quality to that of others, dates back at least to Veblen's seminal work in 1899 (with the notion of "conspicuous consumption"), and was first formally modelled by Duesenberry (1949) who described several examples of interdependence in consumer consumption behavior. In this context, some studies examined the theory and empirical evidence of interdependent preferences such as Akerlof[1] (1997), Alexopoulos and Sapp (2006), as well as Riechmann[2] (2006). The novelty of this essay is to analyze firms' strategies when the market exhibits a social interaction effect in a vertical differentiation model. The quality is assumed to be the factor of interdependent preferences, considering that the consumer compares his/her product's quality to the other products' qualities present in the market.

In the second essay, we deal with addictive goods to account for the effect of consumed quality on consumers' preferences over time. We consider a two-period setting, where the perception of quality at the second period depends on the quality consumed at the first one. This quality can either generate addiction among consumers or make them tired of the consumed qualities. In industrial economics, few authors focused their analysis on addictive goods. Becker and Murphy (1988) introduced the theory of rational addiction according to which, the presence of addiction in a market leads consumers to develop a rational behavior and to anticipate the future actions of firms, which affects the existence of equilibrium and the market's stability. Driskill and McCafferty (2001) used the theory of Becker and Murphy (1988) in the specification of preferences and showed from an infinite game the multiplicity of Markovian equilibria. Our second essay confirms the problem of equilibrium existence when consumed qualities are assumed to affect future preferences. However, none of the previous papers analyzed those effects in a vertical differentiation model. From our viewpoint, this model's type is the most adapted one to take into account the behavior of consumers whom preferences vary according to the consumed qualities.

On each essay, we identify the necessary and sufficient conditions for the existence of the Subgame Perfect Nash Equilibrium (SPNE) and analyze the firms' strategies and the market structure at equilibrium.

Section 2 introduces the benchmark model. Section 3 describes the modeling and the market outcomes when the market exhibits Relative Preferences for Quality (RPQ). Section 4 investigates the market outcome and the equilibrium existence when the market is characterized by Addictive Ordinary Goods (AOG). Section 5 concludes the chapter. All proofs are relegated to an appendix.

[1]Akerlof (1997) proved in his theory of consumer status seeking, that the satisfaction of a consumer increases with the difference between the personal status and others' status.

[2]Alexopoulos and Sapp (2006) as well as Riechmann (2006) investigate the outcomes of the market when firms maximize their relative payoffs equal to the difference between their own profit and the profit of their competitor.

2. Benchmark Model

We consider the standard model of vertical differentiation (Mussa and Rosen, 1978), where consumers are characterized by their intensity of preference for quality θ. They are uniformly distributed on $[\underline{\theta}, \overline{\theta}]$ with density equal to 1. There are two firms competing in the market which produce distinct goods; note p_i and q_i respectively the price and the quality of good i $(i = 1, 2)$. Each consumer is supposed to buy at most one unit of product from the firm that ensures to him/her the highest utility except if the alternative of no purchase is better. The conditional indirect utility of a type θ's consumer is given by:

$$U_i(\theta) = \begin{cases} \theta q_i - p_i & \text{if he/she buys product } i \\ 0 & \text{if he/she buys nothing} \end{cases}$$

with $i = 1, 2$, where $q_i \in [\underline{q}, \overline{q}]$ $\forall i = 1, 2$. $\underline{q} > 0$, is the minimal quality required. $p_i \in [0, y]$ $\forall i = 1, 2$. Let y be the consumer's income which is supposed to be the same for all consumers.

Production is supposed to be costless.

Since prices are more easily adjusted than qualities, it is reasonable to model price and quality competition by a two-step game in which firms choose their qualities in the first step and compete in prices in the second one.

3. Relative Preferences for Quality (RPQ)

Consider the case of two women sitting side by side in the train. One of them wears a Chanel dress, the other one a C&A dress. One may imagine that the woman wearing Chanel feels happy because the quality of her dress is better than her neighbor's one. Conversely, the woman wearing C&A envies the other woman, and may feel sad and uneasy because her dress is of lower quality. The same situation happens for two men who are parking their cars (a Porsch and a Fiat Uno) side by side. These everyday situations happen when consumers seek for some social distinction or for a relative position[3], comparing the purchased quality to the other qualities available in the market. The aim of this essay is to model this particular consumption behavior by assuming that people get worse

[3]Most of the existing work on this topic has used surveys and laboratory experiments to investigate how individuals' satisfaction depends on relative factors such as income and wealth: Clark (2003), Solnick and Hemenway (1998) and Zizzo and Oswald (2000).

when they consume a low quality product compared to another one available in the market and vice versa. We will refer to this phenomenon as relative preferences for quality (RPQ). The phenomenon is added to the standard satisfaction derived from the intrinsic characteristics of products: their qualities and their prices.

Exploring the price and the quality competition in a duopoly between a low and a high quality firms, we prove that the market structure at equilibrium depends on the intensity of RPQ. Under some conditions, the market is monopolized by only one firm, which comes in contradiction with the benchmark model of Choi and Chin (1992) who characterize the equilibrium of a vertically differentiated duopoly when the market is partially covered, and prove that there is always room for two firms when the market is partially covered.

3.1. RPQ Model's Specifications

In this model, we add to the Mussa and Rosen's model (presented in Section 2) a term that reflects the effects of the relative preferences for quality (RPQ). The choice of the good depends not only on the absolute quality and the price levels but also on the level of Relative Preferences for Quality.

In this model, we assume that $\underline{\theta} = 0$, to ensure that the market is partially covered at equilibrium. The conditional indirect utility of a type θ's consumer is given by:

$$U_i(\theta) = \begin{cases} \theta q_i - p_i + \beta(q_i - q_j) & \text{if he/she buys product } i, \\ 0 & \text{if he/she buys neither product.} \end{cases}$$

The term $\beta(q_i - q_j)$ represents the gain or loss in utility resulting from the relative preferences for quality[4] of the consumer who buys the product i. It reflects the happiness (sadness) of the consumer to consume a product of better (lower) quality than the other one available in the market. The RPQ term results from the comparison between the quality acquired by the consumer and the other quality. Thus, β corresponds to the intensity of the social distinction desire. The larger is β, the more important is the impact of relative preferences in the satisfaction of consumers. Later on, we will refer to β as RPQ's intensity.

[4]We suppose RPQ to be the difference between the quality acquired and the other one, similarly to modelling used by Ghazzai (2008) in a multiproduct monopoly setting as well as Alexopoulos and Sapp (2006) and Riechmann(2006) who represent the relative payoffs of firms by the difference between the own payoff of a firm and its competitor's payoff.

The consumer is consciously or unconsciously driven to compare the product that he/she buys and the other product available in the market. His/her purchase decision depends not only on his/her intrinsic evaluation of quality and the product's price (as it is the case of the standard model of Vertical Product Differentiation) but also on his/her relative preferences for product quality[5].

3.2. RPQ's Market Outcome

The quality and pricing game is solved by backward induction, beginning by the characterization of demands as a function of p_i and q_i, for $i = 1, 2$, then, solving the price equilibrium for given qualities and finally the quality choice of firms.

3.2.1. Demand Characterization

We assume that $q_2 > q_1$. Firm 2 is thus the high quality firm.

The demand addressed to Firm i is defined by the set of consumers who maximize utility when buying product i, rather than product j or not buying at all.

Lemma 1. *The firms' demand are given by:*

$$D_1 = \begin{cases} \overline{\theta} - \theta_1 & if \;\; \theta_1 < \overline{\theta} < \hat{\theta} \\ \hat{\theta} - \theta_1 & if \;\; \theta_1 \leq \hat{\theta} \leq \overline{\theta} \\ 0 & if \;\; \hat{\theta} < \theta_2 < \overline{\theta} \end{cases}$$

$$D_2 = \begin{cases} \overline{\theta} - \theta_2 & if \;\; \hat{\theta} < \theta_2 < \overline{\theta} \\ \overline{\theta} - \hat{\theta} & if \;\; \theta_1 \leq \hat{\theta} \leq \overline{\theta} \\ 0 & if \;\; \theta_1 < \overline{\theta} < \hat{\theta} \end{cases}$$

[5]In the case of n firms (n qualities), the consumer who buys product i evaluates his/her satisfaction by comparing his product quality with all the other market's products. In this case, his satisfaction is expressed as $\theta q_i - p_i + \beta(q_i - q_1) + \beta(q_i - q_2) + \cdots + \beta(q_i - q_j) + \cdots + \beta(q_i - q_n)$ which is rewritten $U_i = \theta q_i - p_i + \beta((n-1)q_i - \sum_{j \neq i} q_j)$.

$$
\text{with} \begin{cases} \hat{\theta} = \frac{p_2 - p_1}{q_2 - q_1} - 2\beta & \textit{being the consumer indifferent between} \\ & \textit{buying product 1 or product 2;} \\ \theta_1 = \frac{p_1 + \beta(q_2 - q_1)}{q_1} & \textit{being the consumer indifferent between buying} \\ & \textit{product 1 and not buying at all} \\ \textit{and} & \\ \theta_2 = \frac{p_2 - \beta(q_2 - q_1)}{q_2} & \textit{being the consumer indifferent between buying} \\ & \textit{product 2 and not buying at all.} \end{cases}
$$

According to Lemma 1, we obtain three demand configurations. Either, the two firms share the market, or one of them monopolizes the market.

Notice that the value of θ_1 is higher than the value obtained in the standard model of vertical differentiation, which is equal to $\frac{p_1}{q_1}$. This implies that this marginal consumer becomes more sensitive to the quality and that his/her RPQ's term $\beta(q_1 - q_2)$ outweighs his/her absolute preference for quality θq_1. To explain this result, imagine a consumer who prefers buying nothing even if he/she could afford to buy a Sagem cellular because he knows that Nokia is available in the market.

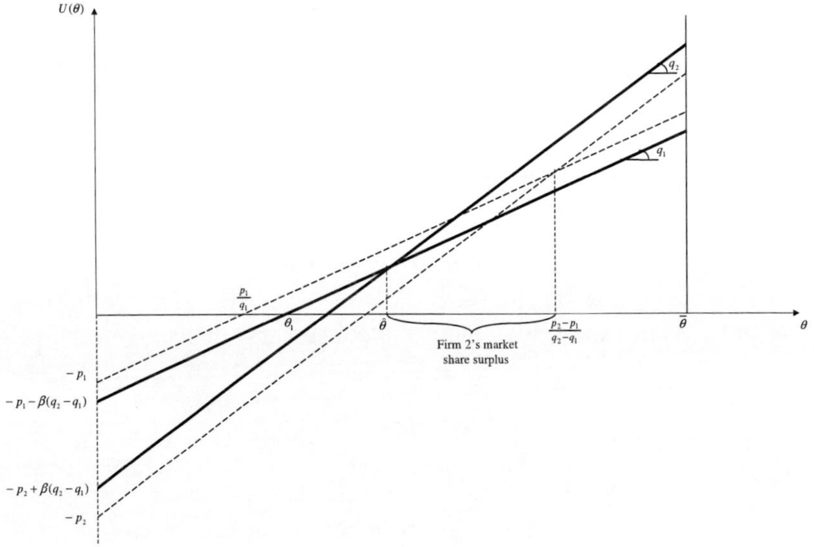

Figure 1. Marginal consumers.

If β is taken to be 0 (no RPQ), the value $\hat{\theta}$ corresponds to the marginal consumer in the standard model of vertical differentiation. By introducing RPQ, the marginal consumer is shifted on the left by 2β, reducing then Firm 1's market share relative to the standard model of vertical differentiation. In fact, a part of its initial market share is lost due to the RPQ of the lowest preference's consumer. However, Firm 2 (offering higher quality) gets an additional market share (2β) which decreases consequently Firm 1's market share as we can see it in Fig.1.

3.2.2. Equilibrium Prices

We solve the step of the game corresponding to the choice of prices for given q_1 and q_2. Since costs are set to zero, the profit function for Firm i is given by:

$$\pi_i(p,q) = p_i D_i(p,q).$$

The subgame equilibrium of price competition is described in Proposition 1.

Proposition 1. *Two cases emerge at price competition equilibrium:*

1. *When* $\frac{q_2}{q_1} \geq \frac{\overline{\theta}}{2\beta}$ *only the high quality firm* (*Firm* 2) *is viable.*

2. *When* $\frac{q_2}{q_1} < \frac{\overline{\theta}}{2\beta}$ *both firms are viable at price competition with* $p_1^* = \frac{(q_2-q_1)(\overline{\theta}q_1-2\beta q_2)}{(4q_2-q_1)}$ *and* $p_2^* = \frac{(q_2-q_1)(2\overline{\theta}q_2+\beta(3q_2-q_1))}{(4q_2-q_1)}$.

We prove that, when the quality differentiation between both firms is sufficiently high ($\frac{q_2}{q_1} \geq \frac{\overline{\theta}}{2\beta}$), Firm 2, the highest quality firm, can push its competitor out and monopolizes accordingly the market.

Exploring further the second case ($\frac{q_2}{q_1} < \frac{\overline{\theta}}{2\beta}$), when both firms are viable at price equilibrium, we obtain the consumers' demands at the price equilibrium as:

$$D_1^*(q_1,q_2) = \frac{(\overline{\theta}q_1 - 2\beta q_2)q_2}{q_1(4q_2 - q_1)}$$

and

$$D_2^*(q_1,q_2) = \frac{(2\overline{\theta}q_2 + \beta(3q_2 - q_1))}{4q_2 - q_1}.$$

Notice that Firm 2's market share and price are increasing with the extent of RPQ (β), while Firm 1's market share and price are decreasing w.r.t this same parameter. Indeed, RPQ have opposite effects on firms depending on the respective qualities. The more consumers are concerned with quality comparison, the higher (the lower) will be the willingness to pay for the product and the market share of the high quality firm (low quality firm).

The main difference of our results with those of the standard model of Choi and Chin (1992) is that the price of the high quality firm is higher than its price in the standard model[6] (p_2^{sd}),

$$p_2^* - p_2^{sd} = \beta\left(3q_2 - q_1\right)\left(\frac{q_2 - q_1}{4q_2 - q_1}\right) > 0.$$

Whereas the price of the low quality firm decreases relative to that of the standard vertical differentiation model (p_1^{sd}):

$$p_1^* - p_1^{sd} = -2\beta q_2\left(\frac{q_2 - q_1}{4q_2 - q_1}\right) < 0.$$

This is explained by the fact that Firm 1 is forced to decrease its price in the presence of consumers' social interaction based on quality to compensate the loss of satisfaction due to the comparison with the higher quality. Firm 2's consumers having a higher willingness to pay for quality as they are more satisfied with the high quality offered, this allows Firm 2 (of high quality) to raise its price and its profitability relative to the standard case.

3.2.3. Equilibrium Quality

We now turn to the first step of the game where qualities are chosen. Solving for the optimal qualities yields:

Proposition 2. *The quality subgame equilibrium depends on β, the intensity of RPQ and on consumers' heterogeneity ($\overline{\theta}$), in the following way:*

- *If $\beta \geq \frac{\overline{\theta}}{2}$,*

$$\left(q_i^*, q_j^*\right) = \left(\underline{q}, \overline{q}\right) \text{ with } i = 1, 2;\ i \neq j,$$

and Firm i is inactive[7].

[6]In the case of β equal to 0, the prices are those obtained in the standard model of vertical product differentiation.

[7]We suppose that the potential competitor's quality is equal to $\underline{q}$ as has been done in the standard model of vertical differentiation (for example Anderson et al., 1992).

- *If* $\beta < \frac{\overline{\theta}}{2}$,

$$(q_i^*, q_j^*) = \left(\frac{(2\overline{\theta} - 3\beta + \sqrt{4\overline{\theta}^2 - 23\beta^2 + 44\overline{\theta}\beta)}}{7\overline{\theta} - 4\beta}\overline{q}, \overline{q} \right)$$

$$\textit{with } i = 1, 2; \; i \neq j,$$

and both firms are active.

In the two cases defined in Proposition 2, the game admits two symmetric couples of equilibrium strategies, given the firms' simultaneous decisions.

It is interesting to notice that in the absence of RPQ ($\beta = 0$), the market is always large enough to allow the viability of both firms (as we always have $\frac{\overline{\theta}}{2} > 0 = \beta$) and that qualities converge to those obtained in the standard case (Choi and Chin 1992) as β goes to zero. However, when RPQ are introduced, an additional condition is needed to allow the viability of two firms, which is $\beta < \frac{\overline{\theta}}{2}$, implying that interdependent preferences must have a sufficiently low level to allow the activity of two firms. One of them sets the highest quality and the other one chooses a proportion of the highest quality depending on the heterogeneity of consumers and the intensity of RPQ.

This result joins the findings of Choi and Chin (1992) in the fact that the low quality firm produces a proportion of the highest quality. However, this proportion is different from the standard analysis of Choi and Chin (1992) and which is equal to $q^*_{(\beta=0)} = \frac{4}{7}\overline{q}$. In fact, by comparing the two equilibrium qualities, we find that the equilibrium value of the low quality firm with relative preferences $\left(\frac{(2\overline{\theta} - 3\beta + \sqrt{4\overline{\theta}^2 - 23\beta^2 + 44\overline{\theta}\beta)}}{7\overline{\theta} - 4\beta}\overline{q} \right)$, is higher than the quality equilibrium of Choi and Chin (1992).

Accordingly, the presence of consumers' RPQ drives the low quality firm to improve the characteristics of its product, given that consumers are sensitive to the social distinction phenomenon and compare the products according to their qualities.

In the case $\beta \geq \frac{\overline{\theta}}{2}$, one of the firms chooses the highest quality $\overline{q}$, for every quality value chosen by its competitor. The latter, getting a null demand and a null profit, is inactive. Thus, an important level of consumers' RPQ evicts the low quality Firm from the market, allowing the high quality firm to monopolize it.

We suppose for the coming analysis that Firm 1 produces the low quality product ($q_1 < q_2$). We define the degree of quality differentiation and analyze its dependence on the heterogeneity of consumers and on the intensity of RPQ when both firms are active in the market.

Corollary 1. *For $\beta < \frac{\overline{\theta}}{2}$, the degree of quality differentiation in the Subgame Perfect Nash Equilibrium is decreasing w.r.t β, the intensity of RPQ, and increasing with $\overline{\theta}$, the heterogeneity of consumers.*

The intuition behind the above result can be outlined as follows. For an important weight of RPQ, the consumers are more sensitive to the difference of qualities between the products in their purchase decision. Thus, the low quality firm is urged to improve its quality and to reduce the quality differentiation with its competitor. This implies that the incentive for quality differentiation decreases with the RPQ.

As for $\overline{\theta}$, the larger is the population's size (large $\overline{\theta}$), the more important is consumers' heterogeneity. As a result, the low quality firm is incited to differentiate its product from the competitor's one in order to have a higher market share.

In the foregoing analysis, we have shown that introducing RPQ in a model of vertical product differentiation has a clear impact on the partially covered market outcome. The most interesting result is that an important effect of RPQ may completely change the market structure from a duopoly to a single active firm. Moreover, under duopoly structure, the presence of consumers' social interactions improves the quality's product of the low quality firm.

4. Addictive Ordinary Goods (AOG)

Medical studies show that a child having consumed sweetened water during the first years of his/her life is more likely to show at the adult age a preference for the sugary taste, more than a child who has not. In the same way, an adult is more likely to control his/her meals composition if he/she had been naturally nursed when baby, than if he/she had been fed with milk in powder. Thus, our taste for a given product depends on our past consumptions and changes over time. We propose to model this consumption behavior in this essay, where we consider that the perception of some quality at a given moment depends on the quality consumed in the past, which may account for addictive or habituation behavior.

The consumed quality may increase the willingness to pay for this quality at the following period, which may reflect an addiction behavior. The consumed quality may also decrease the willingness to pay for quality, which may reflect a disgust or an habituation behavior.

We prove that with the introduction of such effects, the existence of equilibrium is not guaranteed, and identify necessary and sufficient conditions on parameters to ensure the existence of a Nash equilibrium.

We prove that at equilibrium, firms maximize differentiation. Concerning the prices strategy two cases emerge. If the consumed quality increases the willingness of consumers to pay for quality at the second period, firms lower the first period prices to trap consumers. At the next period, firms will take advantage from this consumers' addiction by raising prices. This price effect has been identified by Villas Boas (2004). If consumers get tired from the consumption of qualities, firms raise the first period prices to make more current profits, as in Klemperer (1995).

4.1. AOG Model's Specifications

In this variant of Mussa and Rosen's model (presented in Section 2), we assume that $\underline{\theta} > 0$ and that the income y is sufficiently high to ensure that the market is fully covered.

The utility of type θ's consumer who buys the product i is given by:

- At the first period ($T = 1$):

$$U_{i1} = \theta q_i \delta - p_{i1} = \theta q_i - p_{i1},$$

- At the second period ($T = 2$):

$$U_{i2} = \theta q_i \delta - p_{i2}.$$

p_{iT} being the price of the product i at the current period T, q_i the quality of the product i ($i = 1, 2$) and δ the habit's level:

$$\delta = \begin{cases} \alpha q_1 & \text{if } q_1 \text{ is consumed at } T = 1, \\ \alpha q_2 & \text{if } q_2 \text{ is consumed at } T = 1. \end{cases}$$

At $T = 1$, there are no past consumptions and δ is equal to 1.
At $T = 2$, consumers have bought either quality q_1 at the first period ($\delta = \alpha q_1$), or quality q_2 ($\delta = \alpha q_2$), α is assumed to be positive, implying $\delta > 0$.

To make these hypotheses more concrete, consider two firms selling products of different refined sugar rates and having thus, different qualities. The consumption habit can make a consumer willing to pay more to acquire sugary at the second period. This increase in the willingness to pay for the sugary taste reflects an addiction to sugary represented in our model by $\delta = \alpha q > 1$. By developing a consumption habit, consumers can also get tired from the consumed qualities[8] which is reflected by $\delta < 1$.

Firms' choices occur in a three-step game:

1. In the beginning of the first period, firms choose simultaneously the qualities;
2. Then they compete in prices of the first period;
3. In the second period, firms choose simultaneously the prices.

The qualities chosen at the first period remain unchanged and the discount factor is supposed to be equal to 1.

4.2. AOG's Market Outcome

Proposition 3. *The Subgame Perfect Nash Equilibrium* $(SPNE)$ *depends on the market size and the quality differentiation range in the following way:*

1. *For a large market* $(\overline{\theta} > 2\underline{\theta})$, *under the necessary and sufficient conditions*

$$\begin{cases} \underline{q}\overline{q}(5\overline{\theta}^2 - 2\overline{\theta}\underline{\theta} + 2\underline{\theta}^2) \geq \frac{\underline{q}^2}{2}(\overline{\theta} - 2\underline{\theta})^2 + 9\frac{\overline{q}^2}{2}\overline{\theta}^2; & (C.1) \\ \overline{q} < \underline{q} + \frac{1}{\alpha}(\frac{\overline{\theta}-2\underline{\theta}}{2\overline{\theta}-\underline{\theta}})^2; & (C.2) \end{cases}$$

- *equilibrium qualities:*

$$(q_i^*, q_j^*) = (\underline{q}, \overline{q}),\ \textit{with}\ i = 1, 2;\ i \neq j$$

- *first period equilibrium prices:*

$$(p_{i1}^*, p_{j1}^*) = \left[\left(\frac{\overline{q} - \underline{q}}{3}\right)(\overline{\theta} - 2\underline{\theta}), \left(\frac{\overline{q} - \underline{q}}{3}\right)(2\overline{\theta} - \underline{\theta})\right],$$

[8] In pharmacology, the familiarization to soporifics is a similar effect.

- *second period equilibrium prices:*

$$(p_{i2}^*, p_{j2}^*) = \left[\alpha \underline{q}\left(\frac{\overline{q} - \underline{q}}{3}\right)(\overline{\theta} - 2\underline{\theta}), \alpha \underline{q}\left(\frac{\overline{q} - \underline{q}}{3}\right)(2\overline{\theta} - \underline{\theta})\right].$$

2. *For a tight market ($\overline{\theta} \leq 2\underline{\theta}$), under the necessary and sufficient conditions*

$$\overline{q} \leq 2\underline{q}.$$

- *equilibrium qualities*

$$(q_i^*, q_j^*) = (\underline{q}, \overline{q}), \text{ with } i = 1, 2;\ i \neq j$$

- *first period equilibrium prices*

$$(p_{i1}^*, p_{j1}^*) = [0, \underline{\theta}(\overline{q} - \underline{q})],$$

- *second period equilibrium prices*

$$(p_{i2}^*, p_{j2}^*) = [0, \alpha \underline{q}\underline{\theta}(\overline{q} - \underline{q})].$$

From the equilibrium outcome, we derive two main results related to the equilibrium strategies of firms in terms of prices and qualities:

- In terms of equilibrium prices, firms may adopt two strategies. Indeed, when the produced qualities generate a consumer addiction ($\alpha \underline{q} > 1$), the equilibrium first period prices are lower than those of the second period, as proved in Proposition 3. Hence, in that case, firms give more weight to their future gains and reduce their first period prices relative to the second period ones to trap consumers and to benefit from their addiction at the second period. This dynamic effect on prices has been identified by Villas Boas (2004). The reverse scenario occurs when consumers become tired of the consumed qualities ($\alpha \underline{q} < 1$) as the equilibrium first period prices are shown to be higher than the ones at the second period. Hence, firms make larger current profits by increasing the first period prices relative to those of the second period. In this case, the direct effect on prices dominates as in Klemperer (1995). As a consequent, we may think that in a market of addictive good, firms develop a rational behavior at the first period to guarantee their viability at the following period. This rational behavior of firms is inconsistent with the theory of rational addiction of consumers developed by Becker and Murphy (1988).

- In terms of quality equilibrium, firms maximize differentiation, as in Anderson et al. (1992). However, either for a large market or a tight one, an equilibrium exists only if the minimal required quality is high enough to create the dependence effect.

Figure 2 illustrates the existence zone (on the hatched zone) of a Subgame Perfect Nash Equilibrium satisfying the necessary and sufficient conditions of equilibrium existence[9] in a large market for the parameters values: $\overline{\theta} = 2$, $\underline{\theta} = 0.8$ and $\alpha = 0.01$.

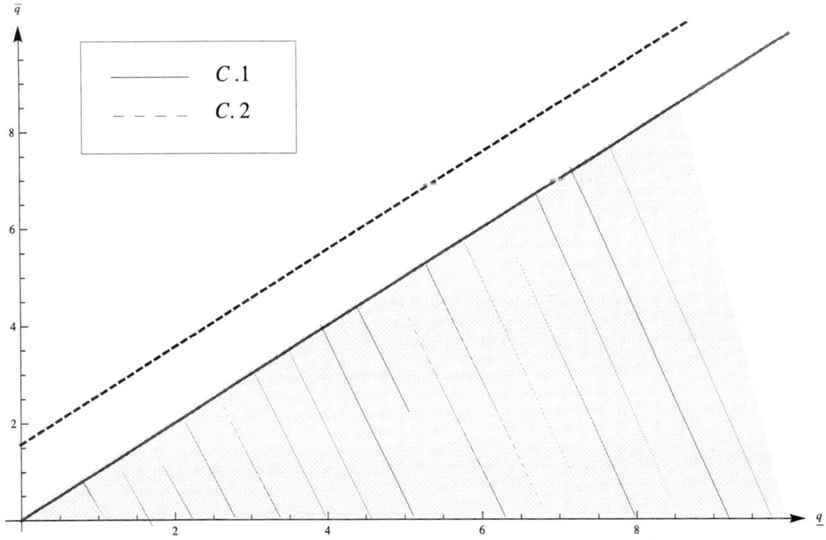

Figure 2. Equilibrium existence in the set $(\underline{q}, \overline{q})$.

The introduction of the impact of the consumed quality on future preferences affects the firms' strategies and the stability of the market as follows:

- The AOG's effect affects the firms' prices strategies. Indeed, at equilibrium, they either choose to reduce or increase their first period prices relative to the second one, depending on the effect of consumed quality on consumers. When the produced qualities generate a consumer addiction,

[9]In Figure 2, we label for the sake of convience $C.1$ and $C.2$, the frontiers of the sets of the couples $(\underline{q}, \overline{q})$ which are respectively defined by the necessary and sufficient conditions of equilibrium existence ($C.1$ and $C.2$).

firms reduce their first period prices relative to the second period ones to trap consumers and to benefit from their addiction at the second period. If consumers become tired of the consumed qualities, firms make larger current profits by increasing the first period prices relative to those of the second period.

- The AOG's phenomenon affects the stability of the market, as an equilibrium may not exist. Indeed, either for a large market or a tight one, an equilibrium exists only if the minimal quality accepted in the market is high enough to create the dependence effect. If this condition is not satisfied, no equilibrium exists, which can be interpreted as a market instability. This is consistent with Becker and Murphy (1988) where the authors showed that an equilibrium may not exist when consumers develop a theory of rational dependence in a market of addictive good.

From this latter result on equilibrium existence and the findings of some other papers dealing with habit formation, we can think that a market where consumers develop consumption habits, may be unstable. To solve this problem, some authors as Bergeman and Valimaki (1996) and Villas Boas (2004) consider an infinite game and solve it by a perfect equilibrium of Markov. Other authors as Reny (1999) aim to find a Nash equilibrium in a finite horizon game by correcting the discontinuity of the profits with respect to the first period prices.

Conclusion

In this chapter, we investigate the effects of the introduction of two specific consumption behaviors in a standard vertical differentiation model: Relative Preferences for Quality (RPQ) and Addictive Ordinary Goods (AOG). First, we account for RPQ when the consumers' utility depends on the effective quality acquired and the other products' quality on the market. Second, we deal with AOG when the consumption of this good's type varies over time according to the quality of the good. This latter quality can either generate addiction among consumers or make them tired of the consumed qualities.

These two consumption effects are not completely anodyne. The main features which may appear may be summarized as follows:

- The number of active firms and the extent of differentiation as for RPQ: in fact, we prove that an important effect of relative preferences for quality may result in a natural monopoly market when the market is partially covered, which is not the case in the standard model of partially covered market where both firms are always active in the market. Moreover, qualities are less differentiated at equilibrium.

- The equilibrium existence and the prices strategy as for AOG: indeed, we prove that the introduction of the consumed quality effect on future preferences in a covered market framework, affects its stability as an equilibrium may not exist, which is never the case in the standard vertical product differentiation model. Moreover, in anticipation of habit formation, prices may be lower or higher on the first period, depending on on the effect of consumed quality on consumers.

Several extensions may be considered for a future research. First, we can test the robustness of our main results by investigating a more general model. For instance, it would be interesting to enrich the model of RPQ by considering that consumers are heterogeneous in their relative preferences for quality, which varies with their effective needs of social distinction. Relative to the problem of equilibrium existence proved in the market exhibiting AOG's consumption, an interesting way to test the robustness of the results is to relax the hypothesis of the market's coverage and allow consumers to refrain from buying when necessary. We can also investigate the same modeling of AOG in an infinite game and solve it by a perfect Markov Equilibrium in order to check the instability and existence of a Nash Equilibrium.

Finally, as we analyzed each effect apart, we may think of combining both of them by considering a dynamical game where consumers develop goods' addiction and exhibit in the same time relative preferences for quality.

Appendix

Proof of Lemma 1.

Define:

- the solution of the equation $U_1(\hat{\theta}, p_1, p_2) = U_2(\hat{\theta}, p_1, p_2)$ as

$$\hat{\theta}(p_1, p_2) = \frac{p_2 - p_1}{q_2 - q_1} - 2\beta;$$

- the solution of the equation $U_1(\theta_1, p_1) = 0$ as

$$\theta_1(p_1, p_2) = \frac{p_1 + \beta(q_2 - q_1)}{q_1};$$

- the solution of the equation $U_2(\theta_2, p_2) = 0$ as

$$\theta_2(p_1, p_2) = \frac{p_2 - \beta(q_2 - q_1)}{q_2}.$$

We easily check that

$$\begin{array}{l} \theta_1 \geq \theta_2 \Leftrightarrow \hat{\theta} \leq \theta_i, \quad \text{for } i = 1, 2 \\ \theta_1 \leq \theta_2 \Leftrightarrow \hat{\theta} \geq \theta_i, \quad \text{for } i = 1, 2 \end{array} \tag{1}$$

For all $\theta \in [0, \overline{\theta}]$, we have: $U_2(\theta) - U_1(\theta) = (q_2 - q_1)\left(\theta - \hat{\theta}\right)$ which has the sign of $\left(\theta - \hat{\theta}\right)$.

Accordingly, and w.r.t the conditions 1, we obtain three cases w.r.t the sign of $\left(\theta - \hat{\theta}\right)$:

1. If $\hat{\theta} < \theta_2 < \overline{\theta}$, all consumers at the right side of θ_2 will buy Firm 2's product ($\theta - \hat{\theta} > 0$). The set $[0, \theta_2]$ is not covered by the market.
2. If $\theta_1 < \overline{\theta} < \hat{\theta}$, all consumers at the right side of θ_1 will buy Firm 1's product ($\theta - \hat{\theta} < 0$). The set $[0, \theta_1]$ is not covered by the market.
3. If $\theta_1 \leq \hat{\theta} \leq \overline{\theta}$, the type-$\theta$ consumers such that $\theta > \hat{\theta}$ will buy Firm 2's product and other type-θ consumers such that $\theta_1 \leq \theta < \hat{\theta}$ will buy Firm 1's product. □

Proof of Proposition 1.

At the price stage, the demand resulting from consumers' choices, given prices p_1 and p_2, are

$$D_1 = \begin{cases} \bar{\theta} - \frac{p_1}{q_1} - \frac{\beta}{q_1}(q_2 - q_1) \\ \qquad \text{if } p_1 < \min\{\bar{\theta}q_1 - \beta(q_2 - q_1), p_2 - (\bar{\theta} + 2\beta)(q_2 - q_1)\} \\ \frac{p_2 - p_1}{q_2 - q_1} - \frac{p_1}{q_1} - \frac{\beta}{q_1}(q_1 + q_2) \\ \qquad \text{if } p_2 - (\bar{\theta} + 2\beta)(q_2 - q_1) \leq p_1 \leq \frac{q_1}{q_2}\left(p_2 - \frac{\beta(q_2^2 - q_1^2)}{q_1}\right) \\ 0 \qquad \text{if } p_1 > \frac{q_1}{q_2}\left(p_2 - \frac{\beta(q_2^2 - q_1^2)}{q_1}\right) \end{cases} \tag{2}$$

$$D_2 = \begin{cases} \bar{\theta} - \frac{p_2}{q_2} + \frac{\beta(q_2-q_1)}{q_2} \\ \quad \text{if } p_2 < \min\{\frac{q_2}{q_1}(p_1 + \frac{\beta(q_2^2-q_1^2)}{q_2}), \bar{\theta}q_2 + \beta(q_2 - q_1)\} \\ \bar{\theta} - \frac{p_2-p_1}{(q_2-q_1)} + 2\beta \\ \quad \text{if } \frac{q_2}{q_1}(p_1 + \frac{\beta(q_2^2-q_1^2)}{q_2}) \leq p_2 \leq p_1 + (\bar{\theta} + 2\beta)(q_2 - q_1) \\ 0 \quad \text{if } p_2 > p_1 + (\bar{\theta} + 2\beta)(q_2 - q_1) \end{cases} \tag{3}$$

Straightforward computations yield the following best response functions:

- If $q_2 \geq (\frac{\bar{\theta}+\beta}{\beta})q_1$ then $\varphi_1(p_2) = [0, y]$.
- If $q_2 < (\frac{\bar{\theta}+\beta}{\beta})q_1$ then:

$$\varphi_1(p_2) = \begin{cases} [0, y] \quad \text{if } p_2 \leq \frac{\beta(q_2^2-q_1^2)}{q_1} \\ \frac{q_1}{2q_2}(p_2 - \frac{\beta(q_2^2-q_1^2)}{q_1}) \\ \quad \text{if } \frac{\beta(q_2^2-q_1^2)}{q_1} < p_2 \leq \frac{(2\bar{\theta}q_2+\beta(3q_2-q_1))(q_2-q_1)}{(2q_2-q_1)} \\ p_2 - (\bar{\theta} + 2\beta)(q_2 - q_1) \\ \quad \text{if } \frac{(2\bar{\theta}q_2+\beta(3q_2-q_1))(q_2-q_1)}{(2q_2-q_1)} < p_2 < \frac{\bar{\theta}(2q_2-q_1)+3\beta(q_2-q_1)}{2} \\ \frac{1}{2}(\bar{\theta}q_1 - \beta(q_2 - q_1)) \\ \quad \text{if } p_2 \geq \frac{\bar{\theta}(2q_2-q_1)+3\beta(q_2-q_1)}{2} \end{cases} \tag{4}$$

On the other side:

$$\varphi_2(p_1) = \begin{cases} \frac{1}{2}(p_1 + (\bar{\theta} + 2\beta)(q_2 - q_1)) \\ \quad \text{if } p_1 < \frac{(q_2-q_1)(\bar{\theta}q_1-2\beta q_2)}{(2q_2-q_1)} \\ \frac{q_2}{q_1}(p_1 + \frac{\beta(q_2^2-q_1^2)}{q_2}) \\ \quad \text{if } \frac{(q_2-q_1)(\bar{\theta}q_1-2\beta q_2)}{(2q_2-q_1)} \leq p_1 \leq \frac{(\bar{\theta}q_1q_2-\beta(q_2-q_1)(2q_2+q_1))}{2q_2} \\ \frac{1}{2}(\bar{\theta}q_2 + \beta(q_2 - q_1)) \\ \quad \text{if } p_1 > \frac{(\bar{\theta}q_1q_2-\beta(q_2-q_1)(2q_2+q_1))}{2q_2} \end{cases} \tag{5}$$

They intersect at $p_1^* = \frac{(q_2-q_1)(\bar{\theta}q_1-2\beta q_2)}{(4q_2-q_1)}$ and $p_2^* = \frac{(q_2-q_1)(2\bar{\theta}q_2+\beta(3q_2-q_1))}{(4q_2-q_1)}$ if $q_2 < \frac{\bar{\theta}}{2\beta}q_1$. Otherwise, they intersect at $p_1^* = 0$ and $p_2^* = \frac{\beta(q_2^2-q_1^2)}{q_1}$ if $q_2 < \frac{(\bar{\theta}+\beta+\sqrt{\bar{\theta}^2+9\beta^2+2\bar{\theta}\beta})}{4\beta}q_1$ or $p_2^* = \frac{1}{2}(\bar{\theta}q_2 + \beta(q_2 - q_1)$ if $q_2 \geq \frac{(\bar{\theta}+\beta+\sqrt{\bar{\theta}^2+9\beta^2+2\bar{\theta}\beta})}{4\beta}q_1$. □

Proof of Proposition 2.

By substituting the equilibrium prices into $\pi_i(p_i, p_j, q_i, q_j)$ we obtain the reduced profit functions $\pi_i(q_i, q_j)$ for $i = 1, 2$.

$$\pi_1 = \begin{cases} 0 & \text{if } \ \underline{q} \leq q_1 \leq \frac{2\beta}{\bar{\theta}} q_2 \\ \frac{q_2(q_2-q_1)\left(\bar{\theta} q_1-2\beta q_2\right)^2}{q_1(4q_2-q_1)^2} & \text{if } \ q_1 > \frac{2\beta}{\bar{\theta}} q_2 \end{cases} \tag{6}$$

$$\pi_2 = \begin{cases} \frac{(q_2-q_1)\left(2\bar{\theta} q_2-\beta q_1+3\beta q_2\right)^2}{(4q_2-q_1)^2} & \text{if } q_2 < \frac{\bar{\theta}}{2\beta} q_1 \\ \frac{\beta(q_2^2-q_1^2)\left(\bar{\theta} q_1-\beta(q_2-q_1)\right)}{q_1^2} & \\ \quad \text{if } \frac{\bar{\theta}}{2\beta} q_1 \leq q_2 < \frac{(\bar{\theta}+\beta+\sqrt{\bar{\theta}^2+9\beta^2+2\bar{\theta}\beta})}{4\beta} q_1 & \\ \frac{\left(\bar{\theta} q_2-\beta q_1+\beta q_2\right)^2}{4q_2} & \\ \quad \text{if } \frac{(\bar{\theta}+\beta+\sqrt{\bar{\theta}^2+9\beta^2+2\bar{\theta}\beta})}{4\beta} q_1 \leq q_2 \leq \bar{q} & \end{cases} \tag{7}$$

Firm 1's profit function:

- If $\beta \geq \frac{\bar{\theta}}{2}$ then, the condition $q_1 > \frac{2\beta}{\bar{\theta}} q_2$ is no more satisfied for all $q_1 < q_2$.

- If $\beta < \frac{\bar{\theta}}{2}$ then, $\frac{\partial \pi_1}{\partial q_1} = -\frac{q_2^2(\bar{\theta} q_1-2\beta q_2)(7\bar{\theta} q_1^2-4\beta q_1^2-8\beta q_2^2-4\bar{\theta} q_i q_2+6\beta q_1 q_2)}{q_1^2(4q_2-q_{1i})^3}$

The F.O.C implies:

$$\tilde{q}_1 = \frac{(2\bar{\theta} - 3\beta + \sqrt{4\bar{\theta}^2 - 23\beta^2 + 44\bar{\theta}\beta})}{7\bar{\theta} - 4\beta} q_2 > 0$$

It is easily checked that $\tilde{q}_1 \in [\frac{2\beta}{\bar{\theta}} q_2, q_2[$.

To prove that $\tilde{q}_1$ is a local maximum of the profit function in $[\frac{2\beta}{\bar{\theta}} q_2, q_2[$, it is necessary and sufficient to show that it satisfies the following conditions:

1. The profit in $\tilde{q}_1$ is positive: $\pi_1(\tilde{q}_1) > 0$

2. The profit's derivative is decreasing on $\tilde{q}_1$: $\pi_1''(\tilde{q}_1) < 0$

Firm 2's profit function:

- For $q_2 < \frac{\overline{\theta}}{2\beta} q_1$,
$\frac{\partial \pi_2}{\partial q_2} = \frac{(2\overline{\theta} q_2+\beta(3q_2-q_1))(2\overline{\theta} q_2(4q_2-3q_1)+q_1^2(4\overline{\theta}-\beta)+\beta q_2(12q_2-5q_1))}{(4q_2-q_1)^3} > 0.$

- For $q_2 \in [\frac{\bar{\theta}}{2\beta} q_1, \frac{(\bar{\theta}+\beta+\sqrt{\bar{\theta}^2+9\beta^2+2\bar{\theta}\beta})}{4\beta} q_1[$, we show that $\frac{\partial \pi_2}{\partial q_2}$ has the same sign as the following expression $(\beta q_2^2 - 3\beta q_2^2 + 2\beta q_2 q_1 + 2\overline{\theta} q_1 q_2)$ which is positive for all $q_2 < \frac{(\bar{\theta}+\beta+\sqrt{\bar{\theta}^2+9\beta^2+2\bar{\theta}\beta})}{4\beta} q_1$.

- For $q_2 \in [\frac{(\bar{\theta}+\beta+\sqrt{\bar{\theta}^2+9\beta^2+2\bar{\theta}\beta})}{4\beta} q_j, \bar{q}]$, $\frac{\partial \pi_2}{\partial q_2} = \frac{(\overline{\theta}^2 q_2^2+2\overline{\theta}\beta q_2^2+\beta^2(q_2^2-q_1^2))}{4q_2^2} > 0.$

Firms' best reply functions:

- For $\beta \geq \frac{\overline{\theta}}{2}$
  - If $q_j < \bar{q}$, π_i is null on $[\underline{q}, q_j]$, then it is monotonically increasing in q_i on $]q_j, \overline{q}]$. Consequently, it reaches its maximum in $\overline{q}$.
  - If $q_j = \bar{q}$, π_i is null. It reaches its maximum $\forall q_i \leq q_j = \overline{q}$.

- For $\beta < \frac{\overline{\theta}}{2}$
  - If $q_j < \bar{q}$, π_i reaches its maximum at $\tilde{q}_i$ $\forall q_i \in [\underline{q}, q_j]$, then, it reaches its maximum in $\bar{q}$ $\forall q_i \in]q_j, \overline{q}]$. In this case the firm i's profit function exhibits 2 local maxima. By simple computations, we find that $\pi_i(\overline{q}) > \pi_i(\tilde{q}_i)$. As a result, the firm i's best reply is $\overline{q}$ $\forall q_j < \overline{q}$.
  - If $q_j = \bar{q}$, π_i reaches its maximum in $\tilde{q}_i$, $\forall q_i \leq q_j = \overline{q}$.

Accordingly, Firm i's best replies for a fixed $q_j \in [\underline{q}, \overline{q}]$ of its competitor is given by:

- If $\beta \geq \frac{\overline{\theta}}{2}$ then $\varphi_i(q_j) = \begin{cases} [\underline{q}, \overline{q}] & \text{if} \quad q_j = \bar{q} \\ \bar{q} & \text{if} \quad q_j < \bar{q} \end{cases}$

- If $\beta < \frac{\overline{\theta}}{2}$ then

$$\varphi_i(q_j) = \begin{cases} \frac{(2\overline{\theta}-3\beta+\sqrt{4\overline{\theta}^2-23\beta^2+44\overline{\theta}\beta})}{7\overline{\theta}-4\beta} q_j & \text{if} \quad q_j = \bar{q} \\ \bar{q} & \text{if} \quad q_j < \bar{q} \end{cases}$$

□

Proof of Corollary 1.

The degree of quality differentiation is given by:

$$q_2^* - q_1^* = \overline{q} - \frac{(2\overline{\theta}-3\beta+\sqrt{4\overline{\theta}^2+44\overline{\theta}\beta-23\beta^2})}{7\overline{\theta}-4\beta}\overline{q} = \frac{(5\overline{\theta}-\beta-\sqrt{4\overline{\theta}^2+44\overline{\theta}\beta-23\beta^2})}{7\overline{\theta}-4\beta}\overline{q}$$

Corollary 1 follows directly from differentiating $(q_2^* - q_1^*)$ with respect to β and $\overline{\theta}$:

$$\frac{\partial}{\partial\overline{\theta}}(q_2^* - q_1^*) > 0$$
$$\frac{\partial}{\partial\beta}q_2^* - q_1^*) < 0$$

□

Proof of Proposition 3.

The solution being given by backward induction, the proof will be split into three parts. In the first one, we calculate the equilibrium in prices of the period 2. In the second one, the equilibrium prices in period 1 are computed. The third one is dedicated to the qualities choice.

We suppose that $q_1 < q_2$.

Part 1: Price equilibrium at the second period

The solution of this step depends on the first period demands:

- Case a: $D_{11} = \overline{\theta} - \underline{\theta}$ and $D_{21} = 0$.
- Case b: $D_{21} = \overline{\theta} - \underline{\theta}$ and $D_{11} = 0$.
- Case c: $D_{11} = \frac{p_{21}-p_{11}}{q_2-q_1} - \underline{\theta}$ and $D_{21} = \overline{\theta} - \frac{p_{21}-p_{11}}{q_2-q_1}$.

D_{11}, D_{21} are respectively the demands for firms 1 and 2 and p_{11}, p_{21} are their respective prices at the first period.

The consumer's utility when buying goods 1 and 2 at the second period in the case a, are respectively given by:

$$U_{12}(\theta) = \theta q_1(\alpha q_1) - p_{12} \text{ and } U_{22}(\theta) = \theta q_2(\alpha q_1) - p_{22}.$$

Note that: $U_{22}-U_{12} = \alpha q_1(q_2-q_1)(\theta-\frac{p_{22}-p_{12}}{\alpha q_1(q_2-q_1)}) = \alpha q_1(q_2-q_1)(\theta-\widetilde{\theta_{II}^a})$ implying:

1. If $\widetilde{\theta_{II}^a} < \underline{\theta}$ then $D_{12} = 0$.
2. If $\underline{\theta} \leq \widetilde{\theta_{II}^a} \leq \overline{\theta}$, then $D_{12} = \widetilde{\theta_{II}^a} - \underline{\theta}$.

3. If $\widetilde{\theta^a_{II}} > \overline{\theta}$ then $D_{12} = \overline{\theta} - \underline{\theta}$.

By replacing $\widetilde{\theta^a_{II}}$ with its value, we determine the second period demand addressed to firm 1 in the case a. We determine by the same manner D^a_{22}.

The production being costless, the profit of a firm i $\forall i = 1, 2$ at the second period in the case a writes: $\pi^a_{i2} = p_{i2} D^a_{i2}$. We maximize π^a_{i2} relative to p_{i2} to get the best reply of firm i φ^a_i.

$$\varphi^a_1(p_{22}) = \begin{cases} \frac{p_{22}}{2} - X\frac{\underline{\theta}}{2} & \text{if} \quad p_{22} \leq X(2\overline{\theta} - \underline{\theta}) \\ p_{22} - X\overline{\theta} & \text{if} \quad p_{22} > X(2\overline{\theta} - \underline{\theta}) \end{cases}$$

Where $X = \alpha q_1(q_2 - q_1)$.
Calculations are analogous for $\varphi^a_2(p_{12})$. The intersection between $\varphi^a_1(p_{12})$ and $\varphi^a_2(p_{12})$ provides the second period equilibrium prices in the case a.

We proceed by the same way for the case b.

For the case c, we begin by calculating the second period demands: D^c_{i2}, $\forall i = 1, 2$.

$D^c_{i2} = D^1_{i2} + D^2_{i2}$, D^1_{i2}, D^2_{i2} being demands addressed to firm i respectively among consumers having purchased product 1 and those having purchased product 2 at the first period.

$$D^c_{12} = \begin{cases} \overline{\theta} - \underline{\theta} & \text{if} \quad p_{12} \leq p_{22} - \overline{\theta}Y \\ \frac{p_{22} - p_{12}}{Y} - \underline{\theta} & \text{if} \quad p_{22} - \overline{\theta}Y \leq p_{12} \leq p_{22} - \widetilde{\theta}_I Y \\ \widetilde{\theta}_I - \underline{\theta} & \text{if} \quad p_{22} - \widetilde{\theta}_I Y \leq p_{12} \leq p_{22} - \widetilde{\theta}_I X \\ \frac{p_{22} - p_{12}}{X} - \underline{\theta} & \text{if} \quad p_{22} - \widetilde{\theta}_I X \leq p_{12} \leq p_{22} - \underline{\theta}X \\ 0 & \text{if} \quad p_{12} \geq p_{22} - \underline{\theta}X \end{cases}$$

Where $Y = \alpha q_2(q_2 - q_1)$.
By the same way we determine D^c_{22} and we provide then the second period profits for the case c: $\pi^c_{i2} = p_{i2} D^c_{i2}$. The functions of profit are not quasi-concave. The first conditions on these profits lead to possible maxima defined on the intervals:

$$I = [p_{22} - \overline{\theta}Y, p_{22} - \widetilde{\theta}_I Y]$$
$$II = [p_{22} - \widetilde{\theta}_I X, p_{22} - \underline{\theta}X],$$
$$III = [p_{12} + \underline{\theta}X, p_{12} + \widetilde{\theta}_I X],$$
$$IV = [p_{12} + \widetilde{\theta}_I Y, p_{12} + \overline{\theta}Y].$$

The possible maxima on the interval I are given by:

$$argmax_{p_{12}\in I}(\pi_{12}) = \begin{cases} p_{22} - \widetilde{\theta}_I Y & \text{if } p_{22} < Y(2\widetilde{\theta}_I - \underline{\theta}) \\ \frac{p_{22}}{2} - \underline{\theta}\frac{Y}{2} & \text{if } Y(2\widetilde{\theta}_I - \underline{\theta}) \leq p_{22} \leq Y(2\overline{\theta} - \underline{\theta}) \\ p_{22} - \overline{\theta}Y & \text{if } p_{22} > Y(2\overline{\theta} - \underline{\theta}) \end{cases}$$

We proceed similarly for the intervals II, III and IV.

The confrontation of these maxima allows as to prove that if a second period equilibrium exists then it is necessarily among these candidates:

$(p_{12},\ p_{22}) = [Y(\overline{\theta} - 2\widetilde{\theta}_I),\ Y(\overline{\theta} - \widetilde{\theta}_I)]$, $(p_{12},\ p_{22}) = [\frac{Y}{3}(\overline{\theta} - 2\underline{\theta}),\ \frac{Y}{3}(2\overline{\theta} - \underline{\theta})]$

$(p_{12},\ p_{22}) = [Y(\widetilde{\theta}_I - \underline{\theta}),\ Y(2\widetilde{\theta}_I - \underline{\theta})]$, $(p_{12}, p_{22}) = [X(\widetilde{\theta}_I - \underline{\theta}),\ X(2\widetilde{\theta}_I - \underline{\theta})]$

$(p_{12},\ p_{22}) = [\frac{X}{3}(\overline{\theta} - 2\underline{\theta}),\ \frac{X}{3}(2\overline{\theta} - \underline{\theta})]$, $(p_{12},\ p_{22}) = [X(\overline{\theta} - 2\widetilde{\theta}_I),\ X(\overline{\theta} - \widetilde{\theta}_I]$,

$(p_{12}, p_{22}) = (0,\ \underline{\theta}X)$.

We test theses candidates one by one to find among them the equilibrium.

For the candidate $(p_{12},\ p_{22}) = [Y(\overline{\theta} - 2\widetilde{\theta}_I),\ Y(\overline{\theta} - \widetilde{\theta}_I)]$, π_{12} reaches its maximum at $p_{12} = \frac{Y}{2}(\overline{\theta} - \widetilde{\theta}_I - \underline{\theta})$ hence this candidate does not correspond to an equilibrium.

We proceed by the same way for each candidate.

For the second period prices' step, we summarize results as follows:

- For the case a, at second period equilibrium, firms' prices and profits are respectively given by:
  • If $\overline{\theta} > 2\underline{\theta}$ then $(p_{12}^{*a}, p_{22}^{*a}) = [X(\frac{\overline{\theta}-2\underline{\theta}}{3}),\ \ X(\frac{2\overline{\theta}-\underline{\theta}}{3})]$ and $(\pi_{12}^{*a}, \pi_{22}^{*a}) = [X\frac{(\overline{\theta}-2\underline{\theta})^2}{9},\ X\frac{(2\overline{\theta}-\underline{\theta})^2}{9}]$
  • If $\overline{\theta} \leq 2\underline{\theta}$ then $(p_{12}^{*a}, p_{22}^{*a}) = (0, \underline{\theta}X)$ and $(\pi_{12}^{*a}, \pi_{22}^{*a}) = [0,\ \underline{\theta}X(\overline{\theta} - \underline{\theta})]$ with $X = \alpha q_1(q_2 - q_1)$

- For the case b, at second period equilibrium, firms' prices and profits are respectively given by:
  • If $\overline{\theta} > 2\underline{\theta}$ then $(p_{12}^{*b}, p_{22}^{*b}) = [Y(\frac{\overline{\theta}-2\underline{\theta}}{3}),\ \ Y(\frac{2\overline{\theta}-\underline{\theta}}{3})]$ and $(\pi_{12}^{*b}, \pi_{22}^{*b}) = [Y\frac{(\overline{\theta}-2\underline{\theta})^2}{9},\ Y\frac{(2\overline{\theta}-\underline{\theta})^2}{9}]$
  • If $\overline{\theta} \leq 2\underline{\theta}$ then $(p_{12}^{*b}, p_{22}^{*b}) = (0, \underline{\theta}Y)$ et $(\pi_{12}^{*b}, \pi_{22}^{*b}) = [0,\ \underline{\theta}Y(\overline{\theta} - \underline{\theta})]$ with $Y = \alpha q_2(q_2 - q_1)$

- For the case c, remind that $D_{11} = \widetilde{\theta}_I - \underline{\theta}$ and $D_{21} = \overline{\theta} - \widetilde{\theta}_I$, $\widetilde{\theta}_I = \frac{p_{21}-p_{11}}{q_2-q_1}$ being the type of a consumer indifferent between $q_1$and q_2 at the first period. We consider the conditions:

$$XY(2\overline{\theta}-\underline{\theta})^2 \geq \left[\frac{X}{2}(\overline{\theta}-2\underline{\theta})+3\overline{\theta}\frac{Y}{2}\right]^2 \tag{8}$$

$$\begin{cases} Y > X \geq Y\left[\frac{9\widetilde{\theta}_I(\overline{\theta}-\widetilde{\theta}_I)}{(\overline{\theta}+\underline{\theta})^2+3\widetilde{\theta}_I(\overline{\theta}-2\underline{\theta})}\right] \\ 6\widetilde{\theta}_I(\overline{\theta}+\underline{\theta}) \leq (\overline{\theta}+\underline{\theta})^2+9\widetilde{\theta}_I^2 \end{cases} \tag{9}$$

$$\begin{cases} X < Y \leq X\left[\frac{9\widetilde{\theta}_I(\widetilde{\theta}_I-\underline{\theta})}{3\widetilde{\theta}_I(2\overline{\theta}-\underline{\theta})-(\overline{\theta}+\underline{\theta})^2}\right] \\ \widetilde{\theta}_I > \frac{(\overline{\theta}+\underline{\theta})^2}{3(2\overline{\theta}-\underline{\theta})} \end{cases} \tag{10}$$

$$Y > X\left[\frac{9\underline{\theta}(\overline{\theta}-\underline{\theta})}{3\overline{\theta}^2-\overline{\theta}\underline{\theta}-\underline{\theta}^2}\right]X \tag{11}$$

$$XY(\overline{\theta}-2\underline{\theta})^2 \geq 9\left[\frac{Y}{6}(\overline{\theta}-2\underline{\theta})+\overline{\theta}\frac{X}{2}\right]^2 \tag{12}$$

$$2\underline{\theta}q_1 \geq \widetilde{\theta}_I q_2 \tag{13}$$

At second period equilibrium, firms' prices are respectively given by:

- If $\overline{\theta} > 2\widetilde{\theta}_I \geq 2\underline{\theta}$ then:

  1. $(p_{12}^{*c}, p_{22}^{*c}) = [Y(\frac{\overline{\theta}-2\underline{\theta}}{3}), \quad Y(\frac{2\overline{\theta}-\underline{\theta}}{3})]$ under the conditions:

  $$\begin{cases} (10) \text{ and } (11): & \text{if } X \leq \frac{Y}{3} \\ (10) \text{ and } (12): & \text{if } \frac{Y}{3} < X < Y\left[\frac{\overline{\theta}-2\underline{\theta}}{3(\overline{\theta}-2\widetilde{\theta}_I)}\right] \\ (10): & \text{if } X \geq Y\left[\frac{\overline{\theta}-2\underline{\theta}}{3(\overline{\theta}-2\widetilde{\theta}_I)}\right] \end{cases}$$

  2. $(p_{12}^{*c}, p_{22}^{*c}) = [X(\frac{\overline{\theta}-2\underline{\theta}}{3}), \; X(\frac{2\overline{\theta}-\underline{\theta}}{3})]$ under the conditions:

  $$\begin{cases} (8): & \text{if } X < 3(\frac{\overline{\theta}-2\widetilde{\theta}_I}{\overline{\theta}-2\underline{\theta}})Y \\ (9): & \text{if } Y > X \geq 3(\frac{\overline{\theta}-2\widetilde{\theta}_I}{\overline{\theta}-2\underline{\theta}})Y \end{cases}$$

- If $2\underline{\theta} \leq \overline{\theta} \leq 2\widetilde{\theta}_I$ then:
  $(p_{12}^{*c}, p_{22}^{*c}) = [X(\frac{\overline{\theta}-2\underline{\theta}}{3}), \; X(\frac{2\overline{\theta}-\underline{\theta}}{3})]$ under the conditions:

  $$\begin{cases} (8): & \text{if } X < 3(\frac{\overline{\theta}-2\widetilde{\theta}_I}{\overline{\theta}-2\underline{\theta}})Y \\ (9): & \text{if } Y > X \geq 3(\frac{\overline{\theta}-2\widetilde{\theta}_I}{\overline{\theta}-2\underline{\theta}})Y \end{cases}$$

- If $\overline{\theta} \leq 2\underline{\theta}$ then:
  $(p_{12}^{*c}, p_{22}^{*c}) = (0, \underline{\theta}X)$ under the condition (13).

Part 2: Price equilibrium at the first period

At this step, firms maximize their inter-temporal profits relative to their first period prices. These profits are given for each couple of second period prices determined at the previous stage. These couples are candidates to equilibrium and not necessarily Nash equilibria.

For $(p_{12}^*, p_{22}^*) = [\frac{X}{3}(\overline{\theta} - 2\underline{\theta}), \ \frac{X}{3}(2\overline{\theta} - \underline{\theta})]$, the inter-temporal profit of firm 1 is given by:

$$\pi_1 = \begin{cases} p_{11}(\overline{\theta} - \underline{\theta}) + \frac{X}{9}(\overline{\theta} - 2\underline{\theta})^2 \\ \qquad \text{if } p_{11} \leq p_{21} - \overline{\theta}(q_2 - q_1) \\ p_{11}(\frac{p_{21}-p_{11}}{q_2-q_1} - \underline{\theta}) + \frac{X}{9}(\overline{\theta} - 2\underline{\theta})^2 \\ \qquad \text{if } p_{21} - \overline{\theta}(q_2 - q_1) \leq p_{11} < p_{21} - \underline{\theta}(q_2 - q_1) \\ 0 + \frac{Y}{9}(2\overline{\theta} - \underline{\theta})^2 \\ \qquad \text{if } p_{11} \geq p_{21} - \underline{\theta}(q_2 - q_1) \end{cases}$$

We determine similarly π_2 and maximize these profits relative to first period prices.

Hence the best response of firm 1 in terms of first period price is given by:

$$\varphi_1(p_{21}) = \begin{cases} p_{21} - \overline{\theta}(q_2 - q_1) & \text{if} \ \ p_{21} \geq (q_2 - q_1)(2\overline{\theta} - \underline{\theta}) \text{ and } (14) \\ \frac{p_{21}}{2} - \underline{\theta}(\frac{q_2 - q_1}{2}) & \text{if} \ \ p_{21} < (q_2 - q_1)(2\overline{\theta} - \underline{\theta}) \text{ and } (15) \\ p_{21} - \underline{\theta}(q_2 - q_1) & \text{if} \ \ (16) \end{cases}$$

With

$$p_{21} > (q_2 - q_1)\left[\frac{\alpha(q_2 - q_1)(\overline{\theta} - 2\underline{\theta})^2 + 9\overline{\theta}(\overline{\theta} - \underline{\theta})}{9(\overline{\theta} - \underline{\theta})}\right], \tag{14}$$

$$p_{21} > \underline{\theta}(q_2 - q_1) + \frac{2}{3}(\overline{\theta} - 2\underline{\theta})[\alpha(q_2 - q_1)]^{\frac{3}{2}} \tag{15}$$

and

$$p_{21} \leq \min\left\{\underline{\theta}(q_2 - q_1) + \frac{2}{3}(\overline{\theta} - 2\underline{\theta})[\alpha(q_2 - q_1)]^{\frac{3}{2}}, \right. \\ \left. (q_2 - q_1)\left[\frac{\alpha(q_2 - q_1)(\overline{\theta} - 2\underline{\theta})^2 + 9\overline{\theta}(\overline{\theta} - \underline{\theta})}{9(\overline{\theta} - \underline{\theta})}\right]\right\} \tag{16}$$

We proceed similarly to provide $\varphi_1(p_{21})$ then we calculate their intersection. Calculations are analogous for the other candidates.

We summarize the first period equilibrium candidates as follows:

- Consider the case $\overline{\theta} > 2\underline{\theta}$. If $(p^*_{12},\ p^*_{22}) = [\frac{X}{3}(\overline{\theta} - 2\underline{\theta}),\ \frac{X}{3}(2\overline{\theta} - \underline{\theta})]$, then prices and profits at the first period equilibrium respectively write: $(p^*_{11}, p^*_{21}) = [(\frac{q_2-q_1}{3})(\overline{\theta} - 2\underline{\theta}), (\frac{q_2-q_1}{3})(2\overline{\theta} - \underline{\theta})]$, $(\pi^*_{11}, \pi^*_{21}) = [(q_2 - q_1)\frac{(\overline{\theta}-2\underline{\theta})^2}{9}, (q_2 - q_1)\frac{(2\overline{\theta}-\underline{\theta})^2}{9}]$ under the condition $\alpha(q_2 - q_1) \leq (\frac{\overline{\theta}-2\underline{\theta}}{2\overline{\theta}-\underline{\theta}})^2$
- Consider the case $\overline{\theta} > 2\tilde{\theta}_I$. If $(p^*_{12},\ p^*_{22}) = [\frac{Y}{3}(\overline{\theta} - 2\underline{\theta}), \frac{Y}{3}(2\overline{\theta} - \underline{\theta})]$ then prices and profits at the first period equilibrium respectively write: $(p^*_{11}, p^*_{21}) = [(\frac{q_2-q_1}{3})(\overline{\theta} - 2\underline{\theta}), (\frac{q_2-q_1}{3})(2\overline{\theta} - \underline{\theta})]$, $(\pi^*_{11}, \pi^*_{21}) = [(q_2 - q_1)\frac{(\overline{\theta}-2\underline{\theta})^2}{9}, (q_2 - q_1)\frac{(2\overline{\theta}-\underline{\theta})^2}{9}]$
- Consider the case $\overline{\theta} \leq 2\underline{\theta}$. If $(p^*_{12}, p^*_{22}) = [0, \alpha q_1 \underline{\theta}(q_2 - q_1)]$, then prices and profits at the first period equilibrium respectively write: $(p^*_{11}, p^*_{21}) = [0, \underline{\theta}(q_2 - q_1)]$, $(\pi^*_{11}, \pi^*_{21}) = [0, \underline{\theta}(q_2 - q_1)(\overline{\theta} - \underline{\theta})]$

Part 3: Quality equilibrium

This step is solved through the maximization of inter-temporal profits with respect to qualities.

If $\overline{\theta} > 2\underline{\theta}$ and for $(p^*_{12},\ p^*_{22}) = [\frac{X}{3}(\overline{\theta} - 2\underline{\theta}),\ \frac{X}{3}(2\overline{\theta} - \underline{\theta})]$, we write the inter-temporal profits:

$$\pi_i = \begin{cases} (\overline{\theta} - 2\underline{\theta})^2(q_j - q_i)(1 + \alpha q_j) & \text{if} \quad q_i \leq q_j \\ (2\overline{\theta} - \underline{\theta})^2(q_i - q_j)(1 + \alpha q_i) & \text{if} \quad q_i \geq q_j \end{cases}$$

We determine the best replies in qualities for the first case where $\frac{\alpha q_j - 1}{2\alpha} > \underline{q},\ \forall\ q_j \in [\underline{q}, \overline{q}]$.

- If $\pi_i(q_i = \frac{\alpha q_j - 1}{2\alpha}, q_j) > \pi_i(q_i = \overline{q}, q_j), \forall q_j \in [\underline{q}, \overline{q}]$, then

$$\varphi_i(q_j) = \frac{\alpha q_j - 1}{2\alpha}, \quad \forall q_j \leq \overline{q}.$$

- If $\pi_i(q_i = \frac{\alpha q_j - 1}{2\alpha}, q_j) = \pi_i(q_i = \overline{q}, q_j), \forall q_j \in [\underline{q}, \overline{q}]$, then

$$\varphi_i(q_j) = \begin{cases} \frac{\alpha q_j - 1}{2\alpha}, \overline{q} & \text{if} \quad q_j < \overline{q} \\ \frac{\alpha q_j - 1}{2\alpha} & \text{if} \quad q_j = \overline{q} \end{cases}$$

- If $\pi_i(q_i = \frac{\alpha q_j - 1}{2\alpha}, q_j) < \pi_i(q_i = \overline{q}, q_j), \forall q_j \in [\underline{q}, \overline{q}]$, then

$$\varphi_i(q_j) = \begin{cases} \overline{q} & \text{if } \; q_j < \overline{q} \\ \frac{\alpha q_j - 1}{2\alpha} & \text{if } \; q_j = \overline{q} \end{cases}$$

Calculations are analogous in the case where $\frac{\alpha q_j - 1}{2\alpha} \leq \underline{q}, \; \forall \; q_j \in [\underline{q}, \overline{q}]$. The intersection between these best replies leads to the equilibrium qualities.

We proceed as previously for the second couple $(p_{12}^*, p_{22}^*) = [\frac{Y}{3}(\overline{\theta} - 2\underline{\theta}), \frac{Y}{3}(2\overline{\theta} - \underline{\theta})]$. The same reasoning is followed for the case of a tight market. □

References

[1] Akerlof, G. (1997). Social distance and social decisions, *Econometrica*, 65, 1005–1027.

[2] Alexopoulos, M. and Sapp, S. (2006). Exploring the behavior of economic agents: the role of relative preferences. *Economics Bulletin*, 12(2), 1–7.

[3] Alvisi, M. (2000). Quality choice, fixed costs and equilibrium in models of vertical differentiation. *DSE Working Paper* No. 437.

[4] Anderson, S.P., Palma, A. and Thisse, J.F. (1992). *Discrete choice theory of product differentiation* (pp. 305–316). Cambridge: The MIT Press.

[5] Baake, P. and Boom, A. (2001). Vertical product differentiation, network externalities, and compatibility decisions. *International Journal of Industrial Organization*, 19(1-2), 267–284.

[6] Becker, G. and Murphy, K.M. (1988). A theory of rational addiction. *The Journal of Political Economy*, 96, 675–700.

[7] Bental, B. and Spiegel, M. (1995). Network competition, product quality and market coverage in the presence of network externalities. *Journal of Industrial Economics*, 43, 197–208.

[8] Bergemann, D. and Valimaki, J. (1996). Learning and strategic pricing? *Econometrica*, 64, 1125–50.

[9] Choi, J-C. and Shin, H-S. (1992). A comment on a model of vertical product differentiation. *Journal of Industrial Economics*, 40(2), 229–231.

[10] Clark, A.E. (2003). Unemployment as a social norm: psychological evidence from panel data. *Journal of Labor Economics*, 21, 323–351.

[11] De Palma, A. and Leruth, L. (1989). Congestion and game in capacity. *Annales d'Economie et de Statistique*, 15/16, 389–407.

[12] Driskill, R. and McCafferty, S. (2001). Monopoly and oligopoly provision of addictive goods. *International Economic Review*, 42(1), 43–72.

[13] Duesenberry, J. (1949). *Income, savings and the theory of consumer behavior*. Cambridge, MA: Harvard University Press.

[14] Dixit, A. (1979). Quality and quantity competition. *The Review of Economic Studies*, 46(4), 587–599.

[15] Gabszewicz, J.J. and Thisse, J.F. (1979). Price competition, quality and income disparities. *Journal of Economic Theory*, 20, 340–359.

[16] Ghazzai, H. (2008). Multi-product strategies and relative preferences for quality. *Economics Bulletin*, 4(34), 1–10.

[17] Ghazzai, H. and Lahmandi-Ayed, R. (2009). Vertical differentiation, social networks and compatibility decisions. *BE Journals of Theoretical Economics*, 9(1), Article 20.

[18] Jeanneret, M-H. and Verdier, T. (1996). Standardization and protection in a vertical differentiation model. *European Journal of Political Economy*, 12(2), 253–271.

[19] Klemperer, P.D. (1995), Competition when consumers have switching costs: An overview with applications to industrial organisation, macroeconomics, and international trade. *Review of Economic Studies*, 62, 515–539.

[20] Lahmandi-Ayed, R. (2000). Natural oligopolies: a vertical differentiation model. *dans International Economic Review*, 41(4), 971–987.

[21] Mussa, M. and Rosen, S. (1978). Monopoly and product quality. *Journal of Economics Theory*, 18, 301–317.

[22] Reitman, D. (1991). Endogenous quality differentiation in congested markets. *The Journal of Industrial Economics*, 39(6), 621–647.

[23] Reny, P.J. (1999). On the existence of pure and mixed strategy Nash equilibria in discontinuous games. *Econometrica*, 67, 1029–1056.

[24] Riechmann, T. (2006). Mixed motives in a Cournot game. *Economics Bulletin*, 4(29), 1–8.

[25] Shaked, A. and Sutton, J. (1982). Relaxing Price Competition through Product Differentiation. *Review of Economic Studies*, 49, 3–13.

[26] Shaked, A. and Sutton, J. (1983). Natural Oligopolies. *Econometrica*, 51, 1469–83.

[27] Solnick, J.S. and Hemenway, D. (1998). Is more always better?: A survey on positional concerns. *Journal of Economic Behavior and Organization*, 37, 373–383.

[28] Tirole, J. (1988). *Théorie de l'organisation industrielle*, the M.I.T.Press.

[29] Veblen, T. (1899). *The theory of the leisure class*. New York: MacMillan.

[30] Villas Boas, J.M. (2004). Dynamic competition with experience goods. *Journal of Economics and Management Strategy*, 15(1), 37–66.

[31] Wauthy, X. (1996). Quality choice in models of vertical differentiation. *Journal of Industrial Economics*, 44, 345–53.

[32] Zizzo, D.J. and Oswald, A. (2000). Are people willing to pay to reduce others' incomes? *The Warwick Economics Research Paper Series* (TWERPS) 568.

In: Economics of Competition
Editors: G. Leismuller and E. Schimpf
ISBN: 978-1-62257-416-2

Chapter 5

Modeling the Effects of Mergers in the Retail Sector: A Parsimonious Multilateral Approach

Niels Blomgren-Hansen[*]
Department of Economics, Copenhagen Business School, Denmark

Abstract

According to EU competition law, mergers that significantly impedes effective competition, particularly by creating or strengthening a dominant position are prohibited. To identify these cases, authorities need a quantifiable model of the relationship between the variables that are affected by the merger and some measure of competition. Furthermore, the authorities must make their decision quickly, rendering deliberate data collection and econometric analyses infeasible in practice. The decision must be based on easily accessible data.

In this paper, a simple model of the interaction between the retail and wholesale markets is constructed, calibrated and simulated based on a concrete case (the acquisition and merger of 250 shops previously organized in a voluntary chain of shops comprising roughly half of the market for high-end cosmetics in Denmark).

Model simulations predicts that the merger would most likely significantly affect retail prices. The harmful effects are markedly intensified

[*]E-mail address: nbh.eco@cbs.dk; Address: Porcelænshaven 16.1, 2000 Frederiksberg, Denmark.

through the possible abuse of buyer power to raise barriers to the market and curb the competitiveness of minor rivals. However, the dominant position is vulnerable if increased profits induce the entrance to the sector of more independent competitors. The competition authorities were justified in conditioning their approval on the removal of contract-based barriers to entry.

Analytically, the main results of this work are the following: (1) In a linear model characterized by heterogeneous products and constant marginal costs, the optimal (Nash equilibrium) wholesale price is unaffected by the structure in the retail sector. (2) The effect of buyer-power-induced quantity discounts depends crucially on the specific design of the rebate scheme: A relative discount on the list price that the independent shops are charged *increases* the average retail price, whereas a fixed reduction relative to the pre-merger price *reduces* the average retail price. (3) Buyer power-induced retail price maintenance (RPM) increases the average retail price. RPM increases the competitiveness and profits of the merged shops only if the producers keep the wholesale prices unchanged. If the producers adjust their wholesale prices, then RPM hurts both the merged and the independent shops and benefits only the producers. The harmful effects on consumer welfare and efficiency are intensified.

1. Introduction

According to the Danish Competition Act, the Competition Council (CC) should validate a merger that does not impede competition significantly, particularly by creating or strengthening a dominant position. The CC may condition its approval on the commitment of the merging firms to take specific actions to remove the potentially harmful effects of the merger. Most other countries' anti-trust acts have equivalent wording.

The formulation requires a conceptual clarification. What, exactly, is meant by 'the competition is impeded'? In practice, most analyses focus on the short or medium term effects on consumer prices. However, as important as this variable may be from a welfare theoretical viewpoint, it may be equally important to assess the effect on the efficiency and the dynamics of the sector in question.

Logically, the assessment of whether the competition is impeded 'significantly' requires a quantified evaluation of the likely effects of the merger. To produce this evaluation, we must build, calibrate and simulate a quantifiable model of the sector involved. The model must be consistent with the pre-merger market facts and data and sufficiently specific to create a quantitative evaluation of the effects of the merger not only the sector immediately affected, but also adjacent up- or down-stream sectors. Equally important is that the model must be sufficiently simple to be useful in practice, given the narrow time limits for the authorities' decision that are stipulated in the Competition Act. Finally, it must be possible to calibrate the model using easily accessible data, i.e. primarily the information included in the material submitted by the merging firms, public statistics and 'guesstimates' from experienced competition economists.

In setting up and calibrating the model several highly simplifying assumptions are unavoidable. This point is not a relevant criticism – it is a condition. The central question is whether the simplifications result in (strongly) misleading predictions with regard to the effects of the merger. This troublesome question should be an inspiration for improving the models rather than an excuse for rejecting consistent models in favor of unstructured market descriptions, general non-quantified theoretic reasoning and impulse.

The model simulation approach to merger effect analyses is not new. Werden and Froeb (2006) provide an excellent and thorough survey of the literature on the unilateral competitive effects of horizontal mergers based on the classical structure- conduct-performance paradigm. See also Hovenkamp (2009).

The contributions of this paper are (a) presenting an analysis of a merger in the retail sector based only on accounting data ('a parsimonious approach') and (b) extending the analysis beyond the short-run case by allowing the number of competitors to adjust to the increase in profits, and (c) considering the effects of the merged company's possible/likely abuse of buyer-power in relation to its suppliers and (indirectly) its smaller competitors. The analyzed abuses are (i) buyer power-induced quantity discounts and (ii) buyer power-induced retail price maintenance (RPM) in the form of guiding retail prices, which effectively are binding minimum retail prices.

2. The Case

In 2007 a capital fund (CVC) bought almost all of the 294 shops cooperating within a voluntary chain called Matas[1]. The shops had previously been managed by 180 individual owners, most of whom only had a single shop. The Matas shops are dominant in the market for high-end cosmetics. Their market share is approximately 50 percent.

[1]Konkurrencerådet (CC) 2007.

Legally, the Matas shops were independent units; thus, CVC's acquisition of the shops was considered a merger. However, the competition was already mellowed by the fact that, collectively, the shop owners held a strong brand, benefitted from joint marketing activities, and bought most of their supplies through a jointly owned wholesale company. Nevertheless, the Competition Council (CC) found that the merger might be harmful to competition[2]. The (limited) competition between the Matas shops is eliminated, when the prices are set centrally; when the suppliers are denied access to the shops; when the merger empowers Matas to make suppliers and owners of shopping malls accept conditions that discriminate against independent competitors and/or raise barriers to entry in the market.

The conclusion that the merger would most likely have a significant effect is supported by this analysis. If the previous chain of independent Matas shops were, effectively, a cartel, acting as a single profit maximizing company, we would expect the Matas shops to have charged higher prices than the independent shops, and the individual Matas shop owners to have had a strong incentive to underbid the chain. The Matas chain would not have been a stable cartel. Most likely, the Matas chain was solely a chain of shops benefiting from a common brand and a joint-purchasing company, as it claimed.

As is the case in most mergers the competition authorities consider, the information about the market is limited. From the material supplied by the merging shops we know that total sales of high-end cosmetics in the 250 shops accounted for approximately 1 billion Danish krones (Dkr) and that the gross profit / price ratio is close to one. In addition, we know that there are approximately ten (mostly foreign) larger wholesale suppliers of high-end cosmetics. Most of these suppliers are considered 'must carry' suppliers. Accounting statistics indicate that the margin / price ratio at the production or wholesale stage is in the order of one.

3. The Model

The first step is to consider: (a) the structure of the retail and wholesale markets; (b) the competition in the markets; (c) the functional form of demand and cost

[2]The Competition Council found evidence of competition among the Matas shops, for example, by selling at campaign prices after a mutual sales campaign had come to an end. The council also found that the prices of selected products were lower in cities with more than one Matas shops.

functions.

This paper is based on the following assumptions:

- all shops are of equal size and evenly distributed geographically
- the brands are considered differentiated products and every shop sells every brands (i.e., all of the brands are considered 'must carry' products)
- the consumers consider the shop services to be differentiated, partly due to the differences in the distance from home
- consequently, both retailers and producers engage in differentiated Bertrand competition
- the marginal costs are constant (and all shops and producers have some excess capacity)
- the market demand function for high-end cosmetics is linear, and
- in the short run, the number of shops is unaffected by the merger; however, in the absence of barriers to the market the number of independent shops is assumed to increase as a reaction to the increase in profits resulting from the merger.

In particular, the assumed functional form (curvature) of the market demand function is likely to be crucial to the predicted price effect of the merger. Werden and Froeb (2006) demonstrate that the predicted price increase in a simple two-firm merger case might be as much as four times higher if the demand function is assumed to be isoelastic rather than linear [3]. The choice of the linear demand function is based on the following considerations: (a) simplicity; (b) the isoelastic demand function's unreasonable implication that the creation of a monopoly renders the price indeterminate (increases to infinity) if the elasticity of demand is less than one, which is likely to be the case in the market for high-end cosmetics; and (c) the fact that the competition authorities have the burden of proof if they challenge the merger. Consequently, the produced evidence should be robust and not easily rejected by the court as being based on biased speculations.

[3] In their example, the logit demand curve is almost similar to the linear demand curve, and the AIDS (almost ideal demand system) demand function is almost similar to the isoelastic demand curve.

Finally, we need to choose a metric to be able to measure the quantity of high-end cosmetics sold one-dimensionally. We will arbitrarily choose to measure the quantities in units that sell at the same price of 100 Dkr. This (arbitrary) metric is in accordance with a specific product, a bottle of perfume, described in the analysis produced by the CC. The implication of one-dimensionality in the measurement of sales is *not* the implicit assumption that one bottle of perfume costing 100 Dkr is a perfect substitute to two bottles costing 50 Dkr each or to one half of a bottle costing 200 Dkr. The brands are imperfect substitutes. The one-dimensionality only implies that the shops are indifferent whether they sell one bottle of expensive perfume or four bottles of cheap perfume and that the margin/price ratios are the same. This simplifying assumption is not crucial for the approximate validity of the predicted effects of the merger.

Based on the limited information available and the above-mentioned (hopefully reasonable) assumptions, we can derive the following pre-merger market 'data': (1) Number of units sold: $Q = 20.000.000$; (2) Retail price: $P = 100$; (3) Whole sale price: $Z = 50$; (4) Marginal production cost: $C = 50$; (5) Number of shops: $n = 500$; and (6) Number of producers (brands): $m = 10$.

3.1. The Pre-Merger Retail Market

The first step is to model the retail market before the merger, i.e. a market consisting of n identical, competing, and independent shops.

As mentioned above, we will assume that the market demand function is linear:

$$Q = A - b \cdot P \tag{1}$$

Each of the n retailers sells all m brands. This assumption implies $n \cdot m$ demand functions. However, due to the symmetry and one-dimensionality assumptions the number of demand functions reduces to n, one for each shop.

The demand function of the ith shop is as follows:

$$\begin{aligned} Q_i &= \frac{A}{n} - \frac{b}{n} \cdot P_i - c \cdot (P_i - P_1) - c \cdot (P_i - P_2) - - - c \cdot (P_i - P_n) \\ &= \frac{A}{n} - \left(\frac{b}{n} + (n-1) \cdot c\right) \cdot P_i + (n-1) \cdot c \cdot P_{-i} \end{aligned} \tag{2}$$

where P_{-i} is the price charged by its competitors, c is a measure of the competition among the individual shops, and $(n-1)\cdot c$ is a measure of the competition that the individual shop faces from its $(n-1)$ competitors.

The ith shop sets its price to maximize its gross profit:

$$\Pi_i = Q_i \cdot (P_i - Z_i) \tag{3}$$

where Z_i is the wholesale price paid by the ith shop.

The FOC is:

$$\frac{\partial \Pi_i}{\partial P_i} = Q_i - \left(\frac{b}{n} + (n-1)\cdot c\right)\cdot (P_i - Z_i) = 0 \tag{4}$$

Because all n shops are assumed to be identical, they are charged the same wholesale price, $Z_i = Z$, and they all peg the same retail price, $P_i = P_{-i} = P$:

$$P = \frac{1}{2\cdot b + n\cdot (n-1)\cdot c}\cdot A + \frac{b + n\cdot (n-1)\cdot c}{2\cdot b + n\cdot (n-1)\cdot c}\cdot Z \tag{5}$$

By substituting 5 for P in 2, we may derive the quantity sold as a function of the wholesale price Z, the number of shops n, and the intensity of competition among shops c:

$$Q = \omega \cdot (A - b\cdot Z) \tag{6}$$

$$\omega \equiv \frac{b + n\cdot (n-1)\cdot c}{2\cdot b + n\cdot (n-1)\cdot c} \simeq \frac{b + n^2\cdot c}{2\cdot b + n^2\cdot c} \tag{7}$$

The parameter ω measures the ratio between the quantity actually sold given the imperfect competition in the retail market before the merger and the quantity sold in the hypothetical case of perfect competition, i.e. if $(n-1)\cdot c \to \infty$ and, consequently, $P = Z$.

3.2. The Pre-Merger Wholesale Market

Similar to the retail market, the producer (or wholesale) market is assumed to be characterized by monopolistic competition. The m producers are of equal size and face identical marginal costs, C. As in the retail market, the symmetry and one-dimensionality assumptions reduce the effective number of demand functions from $n\cdot m$ to the number of producers, m.

The representative jth supplier's demand function is as follows:

$$\begin{aligned} Q_{Pj} &= \frac{\omega}{m} \cdot (A - b \cdot Z_j) - d\omega(m-1) \cdot (Z_j - Z_{-j}) \\ &= \frac{\omega}{m} \cdot [A - (b + dm(m-1)) \cdot Z_j + dm(m-1) \cdot Z_{-j}] \end{aligned} \quad (8)$$

The parameter d is a measure of the competition among the individual producers, and $d \cdot (m-1)$ is a measure of the competition that tthe individual producer encounters from his $(m-1)$ competitors.

Producer no. j sets his wholesale price Z_j to maximize his gross profit:

$$\Pi_{Pj} = Q_{Pj} \cdot (Z_j - C)$$

under the assumption that his $(m-1)$ competitors do not change their prices. The FOC is:

$$\frac{\partial \Pi_{Pj}}{\partial Z_j} = Q_{Pj} - \frac{\omega}{m} \cdot (b + dm(m-1)) \cdot (Z_j - C) = 0 \quad (9)$$

From the assumption that all of the producers face identical demand and costs functions, the common wholesale price Z reduces to:

$$Z = \frac{1}{2b + dm(m-1)} \cdot A + \frac{b + dm(m-1)}{2b + dm(m-1)} \cdot C \quad (10)$$

It is worth noting that the common wholesale price is unaffected by the variables that define the competition in the retail market (n and c), when the marginal costs are constant. The Nash equilibrium wholesale price will be the same if the retail market is characterized by either a monopoly $(n = 1)$ or a large number of competitors $(n \to \infty)$, and if the products are either perfect substitutes $(c \to \infty)$ or imperfect substitutes $(c < \infty)$.

However, the derivation of this conclusion is based on the assumption that all shops are identical. It is not clear that this assumptionit holds true if several of the shops merge because the conditions of the merged shops and the independent shops are no longer identical. This question will be addressed in section 4.2.

Furthermore, the conclusion that the level and structure of the wholesale prices are unaffected by a merger in the retail sector is clearly inaccurate, if wholesale prices are determined via bargaining between the producers and retailers rather than unilaterally by the producers, cf. Mazzaotto 2004. This situation is addressed in section 5.

3.3. Model Calibration

The model contains four parameters to be determined:, A, b, c, and d. However, we have only three independent relationships: The two first-order conditions determining retail and wholesale prices, (5) and (10) and one of the three demand functions: for the whole market (1), the individual retailer (2), and the individual producer (8). Consequently, these three relationships must be supplemented with a fourth relationship.

In principle, one might make an econometric estimate of any of the three demand functions. However, the necessary data are not available. In addition, even in cases in which we do have data and attempt to estimate the price elasticity, the estimate is almost always so uncertain that it does not effectively provide much of a restriction on reasonable guesstimates.

From the margin/price ratio, $(P - Z)/P = 1/\varepsilon_i = 0.5$, we know the price (point) elasticity of the representative retailer's demand curve $\varepsilon_i = 2$. The elasticity of the total market ε is clearly significantly less and most likely less than one.

Our best guesstimate is that the (point) market elasticity of demand ε is close to 0.5. We base this guesstimate primarily on two indications: (a) the CC found that the sale of high-end cosmetics had grown significantly more rapidly in recent years than the sale of low-end cosmetics (and there is no reason to believe that this faster growth rate is due to a decrease in the relative price of high-end cosmetics) and (b) the Dorfman-Steiner condition[4] and the fact that the market for high-end cosmetics is characterized by high marketing and development costs. However, our guess is no doubt uncertain. As a check of the robustness of our central predictions, we derive the likely effects assuming, alternatively, that $\varepsilon = 1$ and $\varepsilon = 0.25$.

[4]Profit maximization requires that the share of marketing costs as a fraction of the price is equal to the ratio of the elasticity of the marketing costs and that of the price. Tesler (1964) finds that the marketing costs as a percent of total revenue are are 3-4 times greater in the cosmetics industry than in the average of 44 consumer product industries. See also Rosenthal et al. (2003) and Fornell and Robinson (1983) for analyses of the relationship between non-informative advertising and price competition.

Substituting ε for $b \cdot P/Q$ and utilizing the descriptive market data ($Q =$ 20.000.000; $P = 100$; $Z = 50$; $C = 25; n = 500$ and $m = 10$) we obtain the following parameter value:

	$\varepsilon = 0.25$	$\varepsilon = 0.5$	$\varepsilon = 1$
$A = (1+\varepsilon) \cdot Q$	25×10^6	30×10^6	40×10^6
$b = \varepsilon \cdot \frac{Q}{P}$	50000	100000	200000
$c = \frac{Q}{P-Z} \cdot \frac{1-\varepsilon\cdot\left(1-\frac{Z}{P}\right)}{n\cdot(n-1)}$	1. 402 8	1.2024	0.801 6
$d = \frac{Q}{Z-C} \cdot \frac{(1+\varepsilon)-\varepsilon\cdot\left(2\cdot\frac{Z}{P}-\frac{C}{P}\right)}{m\cdot(m-1)}$	9444	10000	11111

4. The Post-Merger Markets

The first step is to model the post-merger retail market, i.e. determine the retail prices charged by the merged shops and the independent shops (P_K and P_U, respectively) and the corresponding quantities sold (Q_K and Q_U) as functions of the wholesale pricesthat the producers charged the merged and the independent shops (Z_K and Z_U, respectively). The second step is to determine the wholesale prices as functions of the retailers' reactions to the merger.Throughout this section we assume Nash behavior.

4.1. The Retail Market

We assume that a share α of the n shops are bought by the capital fund and merged and that the remaining $(1-\alpha) \cdot n$ shops continue as independent shops. In this section the number of outlets is assumed to be unaffected.

The demand function of the merged shops is determined by adding the demand functions of the $\alpha \cdot n$ participating shops as follows:

$$Q_K = \alpha n \left(\frac{A}{n} - \left(\frac{b}{n} + (1-\alpha) nc \right) P_K + (1-\alpha) ncP_U \right) \tag{11}$$

The capital fund pegs P_K to maximize its gross profit:

$$\Pi_K = Q_K \cdot (P_K - Z_K) \tag{12}$$

given the wholesale price Z_K and the price charged by the independent shops P_U. The FOC is defined by the following:

$$2\left(\frac{b}{n}+(1-\alpha)\,nc\right)P_K-(1-\alpha)\,ncP_U=\frac{A}{n}+\left(\frac{b}{n}+(1-\alpha)\,nc\right)Z_K \tag{13}$$

The demand function of the representative ith independent shop is only affected by the merger because $\alpha \cdot n$ competitors charge the same price P_K , while the remaining $(1-\alpha)\cdot n-1 \simeq (1-\alpha)$ independent competitors charge the price P_{U-i}:

$$Q_{Ui}=\frac{A}{n}-\left(\frac{b}{n}+nc\right)P_{Ui}+\alpha ncP_K+(1-\alpha)\,ncP_{U-i} \tag{14}$$

Maximization of the gross profit:

$$\Pi_{Ui}=Q_{Ui}\left(P_{Ui}-Z_{Ui}\right) \tag{15}$$

provides the FOC:

$$2\left(\frac{b}{n}+nc\right)P_{Ui}=\frac{A}{n}+\alpha ncP_K+(1-\alpha)\,ncP_{U-i}+\left(\frac{b}{n}+nc\right)Z_{Ui} \tag{16}$$

In symmetric equilibrium ($Z_{Ui}=Z_{U-i}=Z$ and $P_{Ui}=P_{U-i}=P_U$) (14) and (16) reduce to:

$$Q_U=(1-\alpha)\,n\left(\frac{A}{n}-\left(\frac{b}{n}+\alpha nc\right)P_{Ui}+\alpha ncP_K\right) \tag{17}$$

$$\left(2\frac{b}{n}+(1+\alpha)\,nc\right)P_U-\alpha ncP_K=\frac{A}{n}+\left(\frac{b}{n}+nc\right)Z_U \tag{18}$$

4.2. The Wholesale Market

The analysis of the effect of the merger in the retail market on the price setting in the wholesale market turns out to be surprisingly laborious. The derivation is given in the appendix.

The conclusion of the anaysis is that the level and the structure of wholesale prices are unaffected by the merger in the retail sector (and by the pre-merger point elasticity of demand ε).

$$Z_K = Z_U = Z = \frac{1}{2b + d \cdot m \cdot (m-1)} \cdot A + \frac{b + d \cdot m \cdot (m-1)}{2b + d \cdot m \cdot (m-1)} \cdot C \quad (19)$$

This conclusion is not trivial (as it would be if the merger simply intended to divide the market into two separate markets catering to identical consumers). In our case, the merger reduces the competition. However, the two retail channels still compete.

The result depends crucially on the assumption that the wholesale prices are set unilaterally by the producers (Nash equilibrium). If the wholesale prices are determined via bargaining the resulting price vector will reflect the bargaining power of the parties as demonstrated in Mazzarotto (2004). In sections 6 and 7 below we analyze the likely effects of the merged shops' increased buyer power.

5. The Merger Effects as a Function of the Share of the Merged Shops

Inserting the parameter values determined in section 3.3, we can assess the consumer price effect of the merger as a function of the share of the merged shops α. The result is illustrated in figure 1. The graph is drawn on the assumption that the market point elasticity of demand is $\varepsilon = 0.5$. The upper line is the price charged by the merged shops, the lower line is the price charged by the independent shops, and the thick line is the average consumer price.

The graph indicates that a merger that involves less than 30 percent of the shops has a limited effect on the average consumer price. If the merger comprises 40 percent of the market, the price effect is appreciable (slightly more than 5 percent). This finding supports the competition authorities' rule-of-thumb that a merger comprising 40 percent of the market is likely to create a dominant position that impedes the competition. The function is strongly progressive. If the merger comprises 50 percent of the market (as in the case analyzed) the price increase is estimated to be 9 percent, which is approximately three times greater than the price increase if the merger is limited to 30 percent of the market. The authorities' suspicions of the legality of the proposed merger appear to be justified.

Table 1 provides estimates of the effects of the merger on prices, quantities sold and profits. The share of merged shops is $\alpha = 0.5$.

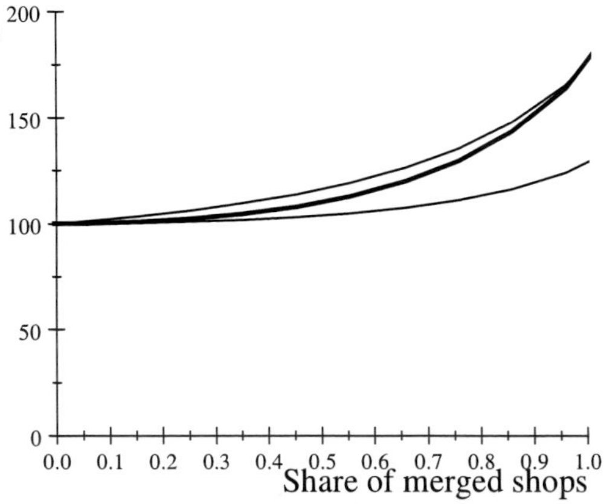

Figure 1. Effect on retail prices of the share of merged shops.

Table 1. The effects of the merger on retail prices, quantities sold and profits

		Pre-m	Post-m $\varepsilon = 0.25$	Post-m $\varepsilon = \mathbf{0.5}$	Post-m $\varepsilon = 1$
P_K	*Dkr*	100	121.7	**116.1**	108.5
P_U	*Dkr*	100	106.0	**103.7**	101.2
P	*Dkr*	100	112.6	**109.1**	104.6
Q_K	*mill*	10.0	8.081	**8.266**	8.782
Q_U	*mill*	10.0	11.225	**10.748**	10.248
Q	*mill*	20.0	19.306	**19.014**	19.030
Π_{Ki}	*kDkr*	2000	2318	**2184**	2055
Π_{U_i}	*kDkr*	2000	2516	**2307**	2098

In the central case of ($\varepsilon = 0.5$) the model simulation indicates that he merged shops raise their price by 16 percent and the independent shops raise their price by 4 percent. The increase in the (weighted) average retail price is 9 percent and the resulting fall in the quantities sold through the two channes is 5 percent. However, the effects on the merged shops' and the independent shops' sales and profitability differ significantly. Reflecting a relative increase of 12 percent in their relative price the merged shops realize a 17 percent fall in sales, whereas the independent shops sell 7 percent more at a 4 percent higher price. As a consequence of these diverging effects on prices and sales the independent shops' profit gain is significantly larger than that of the merged shops, 15 percent and 9 percent, respectively.

How robust are these results with respect to our uncertain guess that the pre-merger point elasticity of market demand is $\varepsilon = 0.5$?

The alternative simulations based on $\varepsilon = 0.25$ and $\varepsilon = 1$, respectively, provide some indication.

If the elasticity is in the low end of the likely range ($\varepsilon = 0.25$), the average price will increase by almost 13 percent (compared to 9 percent) and total sales will fall by approximately 3 percent (compared to 5 percent). The implication for the resulting profit gains is even more significant. The merged shops gain 16 percent (compared to 9 percent) and the independent shops 26 percent compared to 15 percent).

If alternatively the elasticity is in the high end ($\varepsilon = 1$), then the estimated price effect of the merger will be only half as high as in the central case (less than 5 percent compared to 9 percent), whereas the estimated effect on the quantities sold is approximately identical. However, the profit gains from the merger are much smaller: the merged shops gain less than 3 percent and the independent shops about 5 percent.

How critical is the accuracy of the assumed market elasticity of demand in assessing the validity of the merger? That depends on the focus of the CC. If the CC primarily focuses on consumer prices and consumer welfare, then the accuracy is a matter of concern. If, on the contrary, the CC focuses on efficiency (roughly proportional to the decline in quantities sold), then the accuracy appears to be of minor significance.

6. Dynamic Effects of the Merger

So far we have assumed that the number of shops is unaffected by the merger. This assumption is common in most merger analyses but clearly unreasonable in the absence of strong barriers to entry.

We do not know how to measure the hight of the barriers to entry. However, model simulations alllow us to answer a number of related questions such as: How many entrants are required to erode the merged shop's excess profit? What are the long-run effects of the merger, if there are no persistent barriers to entry? How robust are the answers to these questions on the assumed elasticity of market demand?

In doing so we will assume (a) that the market was in equilibrium before the merger in the sense that the gross profit earned by a representative shop, 2 mill Dkr, is exactly what is required to keep the actual number of outlets constant and (b) that the increase in profit earned by independent shop owners due to the merger induces the establishment of new independent shops until the profit has fallen to its equilibrium level.

To solve the model we need to reformulate the equations (11), (14), (13), (16), (12) and (3) as functions of number of merged shops n_K (unchanged, 250) and the number of indepedent shops n_U. The number of independent shops is determined such that the profit of the representative independent shop is back to its pre-merger level $\Pi_{Ui} = 2000$ kDkr.

The solution is given in table 2:

Table 2. The effect of the merger if the number of independent shops adjusts until profit has fallen to its pre-merger level

		Pre-m		*Post-m*	
			$\varepsilon = 0.25$	$\boldsymbol{\varepsilon = 0.5}$	$\varepsilon = 1$
n_K		250	250	**250**	250
n_U		250	293.4	**285.7**	268.3
P_K	*Dkr*	100	110.9	**109.90**	107.1
P_U	*Dkr*	100	98.4	**99.06**	99.96
P	*Dkr*	100	103.2	**103.46**	103.2
Q_K	*mill*	10.0	7.665	**7.940**	8.578
Q_U	*mill*	10.0	12.128	**11.648**	10.742
Q	*mill*	20.0	19.793	**19.588**	19.320
Π_{Ki}	*kDkr*	2000	1867	**1902**	1959
Π_{Ui}	*kDkr*	2000	2000	**2000**	2000

Qualitatively the results of the model simulation may not surprise: The number of independent shops increases, which drives down the retail prices and stimulates demand. However, the quantitative assessement of the effects are noteworthy. In the central scenario ($\varepsilon = 0.5$) the additional number of shops necessary to eliminate the independent shops' excessive profit is only 36 (14 percent of the number of independent shops or 7 percent of the total number of outlets before the merger). In the absence of high barriers to entry it does not appear unrealistic that the number of outlets may increase by 7 percent within a period of a few years.The increased number of shops will reduce the increase in the average retail price due to the merger to approximately 3 percent or a third of the estimated price hike if barriers to entry were unsurmountable. The initial fall in quantities sold is reduced by 60 percent. However, that does not mean that the initial efficiency loss it reduced in proportion. The reason is that the number of units sold per shop falls from 38.000 if the number of shops had remained constant to 36.500 in new equilibrium.

These estimates are rather robust to the assumed market elasticity of demand. If the elasticity is low ($\varepsilon = 0.25$), then the initial price increase is larger, but so is the incentive to open new shops. The necessary accessions of new shops is only slightly larger, 43 compared to 36. Conversely, if the elasticity is high ($\varepsilon = 1$), then the additional number is smaller, only 18.

The loosers are the merged shops. Provided no permanent barriers to entry the simulations predict that the profit per shop eventually falls *below* the pre-merger level, regardless of the elasticity of demand[5]. The fall in profits reflects increased excess capacity in the merged shops as well as declining prices. In the central scenario, the number of units sold per shop is reduced by more than 20 percent.

This development is not consistent with the assumption that the pre-merger profit left no excess profit to the shop owners. The merged shops are forced to react to the declining sale and profit by reducing the number of shops. But it is a loosing strategy. The more shops the owner of the merged shops closes, the more new independent shops will open. This process will continue until the owner of the merged shops is left with a single shop. If the elasticity of accession to the market is infinite at the assumed minimum level of profit per shop (2 million Dkr), then it is simply not possible for any group of colluding or merged shops to earn an excess profit, regardless of size and the market elasticity of demand. The merged shops may be dominant in the sense that it has a large market share. Unless they can impose barriers to entry their market power is temporary.

Theoretically, this result is trivial. The contribution from model simulations is to demonstrate that the number of entrants necessary to erode the market power of the merged shops is rather small and, consequently, that the CC may not need not be too concerned about the merger as such, provided that it can prohibit the merged shops from establishing barrieres to entry in the market.

---

[5]The number of entrants necessary to erode the merged shops' excess profit is only little more than half of the number of entrants necessary to erode the independent shops' excess profit. In the central scenario ($\varepsilon = 0.5$) 23 entrants will do the job (29 if ε is low, and 10 if ε is high).

7. Stackelberg Behavior

So far we have asumed that the merged shops as well as the independent shops take competitors' and suppliers' prices as given (Nash behavior). This is not reasonable. Having a market share of 50 percent the merged shops know and take into account that the price they set will affect the prices set by the minor, independent competitors.

If the merged shops in setting their own price take into account that their independent competitors will react by raising their prices as well (Stackelberg behavior), then the resulting consumer prices will be higher. The interesting question is, by how much?

To answer these questions we insert P_U as determined in (18) into (11) and derive the value of P_K that maximizes the merged shops' profit Π_K and simulate the resuting model.

The conclusion is that strategic behavior matters. In the central scenario ($\varepsilon = 0.5$, unchanged number of shops) the average consumer price is estimated to increase by additional 2.5 percent and total sales to drop by additional 2 percent. The loss in consumer welfare and efficiency is significantly higher than if the merged shops 'play Nash'.

Table 3. The effect of merger in case of Nash and Stackelberg behavior

	P_K	P_U	P	Q_K	Q_U	Q	Π_{Ki}	Π_{Ui}
	Dkr	Dkr	Dkr	$mill$	$mill$	$mill$	$kDkr$	$kDkr$
$Nash$	116.1	103.7	109.1	8.266	10.748	19.014	2184	2307
$Stack.$	121.4	104.9	111.7	7.693	10.994	18.687	2196	2414

However, the most telling result of the simulation is that Stackelberg behavior has a very limited effect on the merged shops' profit whereas the independent shops gain markedly. The reason is that the merged shops' sales drop by additional 7 percent due to an additional 5 percent increase in the merged shops' *relative* price.

This result indicates that short-sighted strategic behavior might not be in the interest of the capital fund that owns the merged shops. Most likely the (small) profit gain is very temporary because the independents shops' increased profit markedly enhances the incentive for potential entrants to open new shops. To avoid complicating the analysis unnecessarily, we will assume in the following that the merged shops take the price set by the independent shops as given.

8. Buyer Power and Quantity Discount

In section 4.2 above we stated (and in appendix we have proved) that unilaterally determined wholesale prices are unaffected by the merger in the retail sector, if the marginal costs are constant.[6].

Nevertheless, quantity discounts that are not cost-based prevail in many markets. Why[7,8]?

An obvious answer is that producers do not peg the price that they charge large customers unilaterally. The producers and the dominant retailer's purchasing manager negotiate, and the resulting price is often a (considerable) price discount relative to the list price that the minor purchasers with no buyer power must pay. The size of the discount depends not only on the size of the order, but also on the relations between the parties, their market knowledge, and their negotiating skills[9]. A large organization is clearly in a much stronger position

[6]Concentration in the retail sector might have a strong effect on wholesale prices, if the concentration in the retail sector induces concentration upstream (Lustgarten 1975). In our case a reduction from ten producers to five would more than double the unilaterally determined wholesale price from 50 to 106. Of course, The CC should consider the risk of a negative effect of the merger on the competition in the upstream sector, but in the case of a merger in the retail market for high- end cosmetics, this outcome is unlikely. The producers of high-end cosmetics have built strong must-carry brands through developing costs and expensive advertising (Tesler 1964, Fog 1994 and Dobson et al 2001).

[7]Buchanan (1952) explains a quantity discount as an imperfect alternative to two-part pricing. Ideally, the producer would like to charge all customers the same price (his marginal cost) and require a fee determined as all or some fraction of the retailers' profits. Two-part pricing would be efficient in the sense that the sum of the producer's surplus and the retailers' surplus would be maximized. However, it is difficult to interpret a normal discount scheme as anything equivalent to joint profit maximizing two-part pricing (Weng 1995). The small retailers pay more than the bigger retailers and fees, if any, go the opposite direction from the producer to the retailers, often as a payment for having the products exposed on the shelves or in flyers

[8]Fog (1994) finds that price discrimination is much less prevalent than predicted by theory. He offers a number of explanations: (i) Price discrimination is considered unfair and harmful to the good name of the producer; (ii) Well-known esteemed buyers abstain from the 'conspicuous exploitation' of their buyer power because they consider it more important to develop stable long term relations to the producer; and (iii) Retailers of 'must-carry'- brands have limited bargaining power.

[9]Fog (1994) quotes a manager in saying that 'our discount depends on the size of the order and the imprudence of the buyer.'

than a small player[10].

Dobson et al. (2001) write that mergers in the retail sector strengthen both the merged shops' market power and buyer power, resulting in opposing influences on consumer prices. Snyder (1996) finds that the merger will result in *lower* prices for both the merged shops and the (minor) independent competitors. In contrast, the CC argues that a discount may result in *higher* prices. However, the CC does not elaborate on the necessary conditions for this phenomenon to occur.

It is not evident how to model the bargaining[11]. Here, we will simply assume that the merged shops obtain better conditions than the minor independents shops. In stead we will focus on the question of the effect of the design of the rebate scheme.

8.1. A Relative Discount

Assume that the merged shops obtain a quantity discount of 10 percent of the list price paid by the independent shops, i.e. $Z_{Kj} = 0.9 \cdot Z_{Uj}$ and $Z_{K-j} = 0.9 \cdot Z_{U-j}$.

In the central scenario ($\varepsilon = 0.5$ and unchanged number of shops) the functions (30) determining the jth producer's sale to each of the two retail channels reduce to

$$\begin{aligned} Q_{Kj} &= 9.917 \times 10^5 + 24546.Z_{U-j} - 27273.Z_{Uj} \\ Q_{Uj} &= 1.289\,3 \times 10^6 + 40910.Z_{U-j} - 45455.Z_{Uj} \end{aligned}$$

The wholesale price vector is derived by maximizing the representative jth producer's profit:

$$\Pi_{Pj} = Q_{Uj} \cdot (Z_{Uj} - 25) + Q_{Kj} \cdot (0.9 \cdot Z_{Uj} - 25)$$

with respect to his list price Z_{Uj}. The resulting FOC is:

$$\frac{\partial \Pi_{Pj}}{\partial Z_{Uj}} = 4099200 + 65456 \cdot Z_{U-j} - 142730 \cdot Z_{Uj} = 0$$

[10] Mazzarotti 2004

[11] The literature offers a number of theoretical, often strongly simplified models in the search of an explanation of non-cost- based discount schemes. Inderst and Wey (2007) assume one seller, one large buyer and a number of small buyers. The producer faces a convex cost function. The contracts between the producer and the retailers are complex and efficient. They share the resulting maximum joint profit. The sharing depends on the buyer power of the retailers, which in turn, depends on their market share.

from which, we deduce the list price $Z_U = Z_{Uj} = Z_{U-j}$ and the corresponding discounted price Z_K that the merged shops are charged:

$$Z_U = 53.048; \quad Z_K = 0.9 \cdot Z_U = 47.743$$

The model simulation predicts that a10 percent discount to the dominant buyer is partially offset by an increase of 6 percent in the list price that the smaller shops must pay. Consequently, the merged shops receive a discount of 4.5 percent rather than 10 percent relative to the pre-merger price (or the post-merger Nash equilibrium price). However, the competitive position of the merged shops improves, and their market share increases indicating that a buyer power-induced discount may be an effective strategy for curbing the competitiveness of the minor competitors. The average wholesale price *increases* by 1.3 percent from 50 to 50.67, and the average consumer price *increases* by additional 0.8 percent (see table 4).

8.2. A Fixed Discount

Alternatively, the merged shops may demand a fixed discount of 10 percent relative to the pre-merger (or Nash equilibrium) price, i.e. a reduction of Z_K from 50 til 45.

In this case, the functions determining the representative jth producers sale are the following:

$$\begin{aligned}
Q_{Kj} &= 9.917 \times 10^5 - 0.9 \cdot 24793 \cdot Z_{U-j} + 0.9 \cdot 57851 \cdot 45 + 24793 \cdot Z_{Uj} - 57851 \cdot 45 \\
&= 731370 - 22314 \cdot Z_{U-j} + 24\,793 \cdot Z_{Uj} \\
Q_{Uj} &= 12.89\,3 \times 10^5 + 0.9 \cdot 67769 \cdot Z_{U-j} - 0.9 \cdot 24793 \cdot 45 - 67769. \cdot Z_{Uj} + 24793 \cdot 45 \\
&= 1400900 + 60992 \cdot Z_{U-j} - 67769 \cdot Z_{Uj}
\end{aligned}$$

Maximization of the profit:

$$\Pi_{Pj} = Q_{Kj} \cdot (45 - 25) + Q_{Uj} \cdot (Z_{Uj} - 25)$$

with respect to Z_{Uj} provides the FOC:

$$\frac{\partial \Pi_{Pj}}{\partial Z_{Uj}} = 24\,793 \cdot (45 - 25) + 1400900 + 60992 \cdot Z_{U-j} - 67769 \cdot Z_{Uj} - 67769 \cdot (Z_{Uj} - 25) = 0$$

which in symmetric equilibrium reduces to:

$$Z_U = 48.\,171$$

The simulation predicts that a fixed discount reduces the wholesale price for both the dominant buyer, who exerts buyer power, *and* the minor players. The reason is that the discount to the merged shops makes the producers earn less from selling a unit to the merged shops than to the independent shops. Consequently, the producers want to sell more to the independent shops and lower Z_U to do so.

Table 4 summarizes the estimated effects of a buyer power-induced discount. The row marked N reproduces the results in case of Nash behavior. The row marked R represents the solution if the merged shops obtain a relative (proportional) quantity discount of 10 percent of the list price and the row marked F represents the solution if the merged shops obtain a fixed discount of 10 percent of the pre-merger price.

Table 4. The effects of a relative discount (R) and a fixed discount (F)

	P_K Dkr	P_U Dkr	P Dkr	Q_K $mill$	Q_U $mill$	Q $mill$	Π_{Ki} $kDkr$	Π_{Ui} $kDkr$	Π_{Pj} $kDkr$
N	116.1	103.7	109.1	8.26	10.74	19.00	2186	2309	47381
R	115.5	105.5	110.0	8.47	10.48	18.95	2296	2198	48664
F	113.1	101.9	106.8	8.51	10.74	19.25	2318	2309	41911

In contrast to the case of a relative discount a fixed discount is beneficial for the consumers by reducing the average retail price by slightly more than 2 percent.

Consequently, if the parties agree on a discount scheme that is designed as a fixed rebate relative to the pre-merger price, Snyder is correct in conjecturing that the isolated effect of buyer power is beneficial to the consumers. However, Dobson's stronger allegation that the beneficial effect from buyer power might outbalance the harmful effect from market power is not substantiated in this exercise. A rough calculation indicates that, in our case, the discount should be of the order of 40 percent for this to occur.

A fixed discount and the resulting lower retail prices may appear an unlikely outcome. The design of the rebate scheme is determined either unilaterally by the producers or as the result of negotiations between the producers and the merged shops' purchasing manager. The model sumulation indicates that the producers have a strong interest in offering a proportional (relative) discount that actually increases their profit rather than a fixed discount that is a severe financial burden. For the merged shops a relative discount a relative discount is also preferable because it is an effective strategy for reducing the incentive for entrants to open new shops.

Consequently, in our case the beneficial effect for the consumers of buyer power that Snyder, Dobson and Mazzaroti imagine is a mirage. On the contrary, the CC are correct in conjecturing that a buyer power-induced quantity discount is harmfull to consumer welfare as well as the competition.

9. Retail Price Maintenance

The request for a significant quantity discount is one way in which the merged shops may exploit their buyer power. Another and more sophisticated (ab)use of buyer power is to persuade the producers to raise their guiding retail prices and put pressure on the smaller, independent shops not to underbid the guiding retail prices, at least not significantly and/or systematically so thereby curbing the independent shops' ability to compete.[12].

Assume that the merged shops demand that the producers refuse to sell to the independent shops that charge a retail price below a guiding price of , say, $P_U^* = 110$ Dkr. This price is significantly above the price that the independent shops would charge in Nash equilibrium ($PU = 103.7$ Dkr) but also significantly below the price charged by the merged shops ($P_K = 116.1$ Dkr.). The Competition Act prohibits retail price maintenance (RPM), but not guiding retail prices. A guiding retail price at this level is unlikely to provoke reaction from the competition authorities. If they should worry about the possible harmful effects and conduct an analysis of the market, they would most likely conclude that the prices charged by the merged shops and the independent shops differ significantly and argue that this fact is a strong indication of effective competition and, consequently, that the guiding prices are not harmful to the consumers.

9.1. Unchanged Wholesale Prices

The effect of binding minimum retail prices depends crucially on whether the producers keep wholesale prices constant or adjust wholesale prices to reflect the changed market conditions.

[12]See Dobson et al. (2001) and Gilligan (1986). The Danish Competition Council (2007) mentions the possibility that the suppliers react to a merger in the retail sector and the resulting increase in consumer prices by raising their guiding prices on their own initiative.

In our central scenario ($\varepsilon = 0.5$, unchanged number of shops) the binding retail price ($P_U^* = 110$) reduces the merged shops' and the independent shops demand functions, (11) and (17), respectively, to the following:

$$
\begin{aligned}
Q_K &= 1.5 \times 10^7 - 125000 \cdot P_K + 75000 \cdot P_U^* = 23250000 - 125000 \cdot P_K \\
Q_U &= 1.5 \times 10^7 + 75000 \cdot P_K - 125000 \cdot P_U^* = 1250000 + 75000 \cdot P_K
\end{aligned}
$$

If the wholesale price that the merged shops are charged remains constant, $Z_K = 50$, then the merged shops' profit maximing retail price is:

$$P_K = \frac{23250000}{2 \cdot 125000} + \frac{1}{2} \cdot Z_K = 118$$

The model simulation indicates that RPM is beneficial to both the merged shops, which sell 3 percent more to at a slightly higher price, and the independent shops, which sell 6 percent less at a 6 percent higher price (see table 5 below). The explanation why it is beneficial to the independent shops to be 'forced' to raise their price is that the binding minimum price effectively makes the independent shops act as a cartel. The difference is that a cartel organized by the independent shops themselves would have been unstable because each of the 250 independent shops would have a strong incentive to not to comply with an agreed cartel price, and the cartel would have no means to sanction the non-compliers. In the case of RPM, the 'cartel' members are policed by the producers.

The losers are the consumers and the producers. The average retail price increases by almost 5 percent more than in Nash equilibrium and total sales fall by additional 2 percent. The profit earned by the producers fall in proportion if, as assumed in this subsection, the producers keep wholesale prices unchanged.

9.2. Adjusted Wholesale Prices.

But why should they? The assumption that the producers should keep wholesale prices unchanged in case of RPM appears unrreasonable. From the viewpoint of the individual producer, the independent shops' demand becomes less elastic because these shops will not raise their retail prices in response to an increase in the wholesale price (up to a level at which the optimum retail price exceeds the minimum price). Thus, theoretically we deduce that producers will react to

RPM by raising their wholesale prices. The interesting question for the CC to consider is by how much.

To assess this question we rewrite

$$\begin{bmatrix} P_K \\ P_U \end{bmatrix} = \begin{bmatrix} 79.340 \\ 64.463 \end{bmatrix} + \begin{bmatrix} 0.573720 & 0.19834 \\ 0.12397 & 0.66116 \end{bmatrix} \begin{bmatrix} Z_K \\ Z_U \end{bmatrix} \tag{20}$$

to expresss P_K and Z_U as functions of $P_U^* = 110$:

$$\begin{aligned} Z_U &= 1.5125 \cdot P_U^* - 0.1875 \cdot Z_K - 97.5 = 68.875 - 0.1875 \cdot Z_K \quad (21) \\ P_K &= 60 + 0.5 \cdot Z_K + 0.3 \cdot P_U^* = 93 + 0.5 \cdot Z_K \end{aligned}$$

Substituting $68.875 - 0.1875 \cdot Z_K$ for Z_U reduces (23) to the following:

$$\begin{bmatrix} Q_K \\ Q_U \end{bmatrix} = \begin{bmatrix} 1.162\,5 \times 10^7 - 62500 \cdot Z_K \\ 8.225 \times 10^6 + 37500 \cdot Z_K \end{bmatrix} \tag{22}$$

The jth representative producer's sales to the merged shops and the independent shops are given by:

$$\begin{aligned} Q_{Kj} &= 1.162\,5 \times 10^6 - 62500 \cdot Z_{Kj} + 0.9 \cdot 62500 \cdot Z_{K-j} \\ Q_{Uj} &= 8.225 \times 10^5 + 37500 \cdot Z_{Kj} - 0.9 \cdot 37500 \cdot Z_{K-j} \end{aligned}$$

Maximizing the jth producers profit

$$\Pi_{Pj} = Q_{Kj} \cdot (Z_{Kj} - 25) + Q_{Uj} \cdot (68.875 - 0.187\,5 Z_{Kj} - 25)$$

with respect to the wholesale price that he charges the merged shops, Z_{Kj}, result in the FOC:

$$\begin{aligned} \frac{\partial \Pi_{Pj}}{\partial Z_{Kj}} &= 0 = 1.162\,5 \times 10^6 - 62500 \cdot Z_{Kj} + 0.9 \cdot 62500 \cdot Z_{K-j} - 62500 \cdot (Z_{Kj} - 25) \\ &\quad -0.187\,5 \cdot \left(8.225 \times 10^5 + 37500 \cdot Z_{Kj} - 0.9 \cdot 37500 \cdot Z_{K-j}\right) \\ &\quad +37500 \cdot (68.875 - 0.187\,5 Z_{Kj} - 25) \end{aligned}$$

which in symmetric equilibrium $(Z_{Kj} = Z_{K-j} = Z_K)$ reduces to $Z_K = 55.124$. As conjectured, the wholesale price that the independent shops are charged is even higher, $Z_U = 68.875 - 0.187\,5 \cdot Z_K = 58.539$.

The effect on retail prices, sales and profit of RPM is given in table 5. The row marked 'RPM fixed' refers to the case where the wholesale prices remain unaffected, and 'RPM adj'. to the case where the producers react to the RPM by raising the wholesale prices.

Table 5. The effect of the merger in case of retail price maintenence

	P_K Dkr	P_U Dkr	P Dkr	Q_K $mill$	Q_U $mill$	Q $mill$	Π_{Ki} $kDkr$	Π_{Ui} $kDkr$	Π_{Pj} $kDkr$
Nash	116.1	103.7	109.1	8.26	10.74	19.00	2186	2309	47381
RPM fixed	118.0	110.0	113.7	8.50	10.10	18.60	2312	2424	46500
RPM adj.	120.6	110.0	114.7	8.18	10.29	18.47	2141	2119	59159

The simulation predicts that buyer power-induced binding minimum retail prices may increase the negative effects of the proposed merger on consumer welfare and the efficiency significantly .

Buyer power-induced RPM is especially harmful to consumers if the producers adjust wholesale prices to 'expropriate' most of the increase in the total profits resulting from the merger.

However, the most salient prediction is that RPM results in the merged shops being slightly (2 percent) worse off and the independent shops being significantly worse off (8 percent) worse off than in Nash equilibrium if producers adjust their wholesale prices, in contrast to the case in which wholesale proces are assumed unaffected.

One might conclude that the merged shops' possible (ab)use of buyer power to force the producers to impose and police the minimum guiding prices in order to curb the competitiveness of the independent competitors is an unrealistic scenario because they should know that the producers have a strong incentive to adjust wholesale prices and that, if the producers do so, the merged shops stand to lose.This inference is likely too optimistic and based on the assumption that the merged shops are sufficiently sophisticated to realize that the immediate gain (at unchanged wholesale prices) is turned into a loss when, eventually, the producers adjust their prices.

Conversely, the 'morale' is that RPM in the form of effectively binding 'guiding' retail prices is a risk that the competition authorities should consider when assessing a proposed merger, regardless of whether the RPM is induced by the merged shops' buyer power or initiated by the producers themselves as a response to increased retail prices.

In Denmark, retailers of luxury specialties appear to be 'disciplined' to a degree that resembles tacit collusion.The problem is attenuated by the fact that the competition authorities have limited means of sanctioning (legal) guiding prices that support and are supported by tacit collusion. Guiding retail prices are likely the most sincere competition problem in the trade in specialties.

Conclusion

In the case analyzed in this paper the Danish Competition Council decided not to prohibit the merger of approximately 250 shops previously organized in a voluntary chain even though the shops with a share of around 50 percent were already dominant in the market for high-end cosmetics and the merger would almost by definition strengthen their dominant position and impede the competition. The acceptance of the merger was conditioned on the removal of certain contract-based covenants in restraint of trade.

The purpose of this paper is not to criticize the decision as such but call attention to the weak analytical premises for the decision. The material on which the decision was made presented several relevant reflections but practically no quantitative assessment of the likely effects of the merger. This is a problem as the wording of the Competition Act implies a quantitative assessment of whether the merger impedes the competition 'significantly'.

The reason for the inadequate quantitative analysis is likely not only lack of data and time but equally much the analysts' reluctance to engage in consistent quantitative modeling because this activity unavoidably and mercilessly reveals to themselves and opponents the shaky foundation of their recommendations.

As convincingly argued by prominent antitrust economist like Werden and Froeb and others the way to improve the basis for decisions in merger cases is to build, calibrate and simulate quantitative models. Models provide analytical consistency to predictions.

The model presented in this paper adds to the literature by being parsimonious in its data requirements and, nevertheless, allowing quantitative assessment of not only the static unilateral effects of the merger but also of the likely dynamic effects and the strategic interaction between the retail sector and the wholesale sector.

The conclusion is that the merger of the 250 shops in the Danish market for high-end cosmetics has the potential of being harmful to the consumers by raising retail prices. However, it also demonstrates that the market power of the merged shops is vulnerable to attack from the opening of new shops induced by increased profit due to the merger. The number of entrants required to erode excess profit appears surprisingly low. As a consequence the merged shops are likely to pursue a strategy of (ab)using their buyer power to curb the independent shop's ability to compete and raise entry barriers. The analysis indicates that buyer power-induced quantity discounts and retail price maintenance may be effective defensive strategies and have severe negative effects on consumer welfare, efficiency and market dynamics. The likely increased prevalence of these phenomena should be a matter of concern for the competition authorities.

Appendix

The effect on a merger in the retail sector on unilaterally determined wholesale prices.

The two retail market demand equations 11 and 14 , and the two retail market price equations, 13 and 18, may be conveniently reformulated as the following:

$$\begin{aligned} \begin{bmatrix} Q_K \\ Q_U \end{bmatrix} &= A \cdot \begin{bmatrix} \alpha \\ 1-\alpha \end{bmatrix} - \Phi \cdot \begin{bmatrix} P_K \\ P_U \end{bmatrix} \\ \Phi &\equiv \begin{bmatrix} (b \cdot \alpha + h) & -h \\ -h & (b \cdot (1-\alpha) + h) \end{bmatrix} \\ h &\equiv \alpha \cdot (1-\alpha) \cdot n^2 \cdot c \end{aligned} \tag{23}$$

and

$$\begin{aligned} \begin{bmatrix} P_K \\ P_U \end{bmatrix} &= \Gamma^{-1} \cdot \left[A \cdot \begin{bmatrix} \alpha \\ 1-\alpha \end{bmatrix} + \Lambda \cdot \begin{bmatrix} Z_K \\ Z_U \end{bmatrix} \right] \\ \Gamma &\equiv \begin{bmatrix} 2 \cdot (\alpha \cdot b + h) & -h \\ -h & 2 \cdot b \cdot (1-\alpha) + \left(1 + \frac{1}{\alpha}\right) \cdot h \end{bmatrix} \\ \Lambda &\equiv \begin{bmatrix} (\alpha \cdot b + h) & 0 \\ 0 & \left((1-\alpha) \cdot b + \frac{h}{\alpha}\right) \end{bmatrix} \end{aligned} \tag{24}$$

From 23 and 24 we derive the demand faced by the two retail channels as functions of wholesale prices

$$\begin{bmatrix} Q_K \\ Q_U \end{bmatrix} = A \cdot \begin{bmatrix} \Sigma_K \\ \Sigma_U \end{bmatrix} - \begin{bmatrix} \Omega_{KK} & \Omega_{KU} \\ \Omega_{UK} & \Omega_{UU} \end{bmatrix} \cdot \begin{bmatrix} Z_K \\ Z_U \end{bmatrix} \quad (25)$$

$$\begin{bmatrix} \Sigma_K \\ \Sigma_U \end{bmatrix} \equiv \left[I - \Phi \cdot \Gamma^{-1}\right] \begin{bmatrix} \alpha \\ 1-\alpha \end{bmatrix} = \theta \cdot \begin{bmatrix} 2\alpha\,(h+b\alpha) \\ 2h + 2b\alpha - h\alpha - 2b\alpha^2 \end{bmatrix} \quad (26)$$

$$\theta \equiv \frac{h + b\alpha - b\alpha^2}{\alpha \cdot \Delta_\Gamma}$$

$$\begin{bmatrix} \Omega_{KK} & \Omega_{KU} \\ \Omega_{UK} & \Omega_{UU} \end{bmatrix} \equiv \Phi \cdot \Gamma^{-1}\Lambda \quad (27)$$

$$= \theta \begin{bmatrix} (h+b\alpha)\,(h+2b\alpha) & -h\,(h+b\alpha) \\ -h\,(h+b\alpha) & 2bh + h^2 + 2b^2\alpha - 2b^2\alpha^2 \end{bmatrix} \quad (28)$$

By comparing 26 and 27 we realize that

$$\begin{bmatrix} \Sigma_K \\ \Sigma_U \end{bmatrix} = \frac{1}{b} \cdot \begin{bmatrix} \Omega_{KK} & \Omega_{KU} \\ \Omega_{UK} & \Omega_{UU} \end{bmatrix} \cdot \begin{bmatrix} 1 \\ 1 \end{bmatrix} \quad (29)$$
$$\Omega_{KU} = \Omega_{UK}$$

and, consequently, that the demand system 25 reduces to

$$\begin{bmatrix} Q_K \\ Q_U \end{bmatrix} = \frac{1}{b} \cdot \begin{bmatrix} \Omega_{KK} & \Omega_{KU} \\ \Omega_{UK} & \Omega_{UU} \end{bmatrix} \cdot \begin{bmatrix} A - b \cdot Z_K \\ A - b \cdot Z_U \end{bmatrix} \quad (30)$$

which is the two-dimensional equivalent to 6.

The representative jth producer sells to both the merged shops and the independent shops. The corresponding demand functions are

$$\begin{bmatrix} Q_{K_j} \\ Q_{U_j} \end{bmatrix} = \frac{1}{bm} \begin{bmatrix} \Omega_{KK} & \Omega_{KU} \\ \Omega_{UK} & \Omega_{UU} \end{bmatrix} \begin{bmatrix} A - (b+e)\,Z_{Kj} + eZ_{K-j} \\ A - (b+e)\,Z_{Uj} + eZ_{U-j} \end{bmatrix} \quad (31)$$
$$e \equiv dm\,(m-1)$$

By maximizing his profit

$$\Pi_{Pj} = Q_{Kj} \cdot (Z_{Kj} - C) + Q_{Uj} \cdot (Z_{Uj} - C) \quad (32)$$

with respect to Z_{Kj} og Z_{Uj},we derive the two first-order conditions

$$Q_{Kj} - \Omega_{KK} \cdot \frac{b+e}{b \cdot m} \cdot (Z_{Kj} - C) - \Omega_{UK} \cdot \frac{b+e}{b \cdot m} \cdot (Z_{Uj} - C) = 0 \quad (33)$$
$$Q_{Uj} - \Omega_{KU} \cdot \frac{b+e}{b \cdot m} \cdot (Z_{Kj} - C) - \Omega_{UU} \cdot \frac{b+e}{b \cdot m} \cdot (Z_{Uj} - C) = 0$$

In symmetric equilibrium $(Z_{Kj} = Z_{K-j} = Z_K \text{ and } Z_{Uj} = Z_{U-j} = Z_U)$ 33 reduces to

$$\begin{aligned}(\Omega_{KK} + \Omega_{UK}) \cdot (A + (b+e) \cdot C) &= (2b+e) \cdot (\Omega_{KK} \cdot Z_K + \Omega_{KU} \cdot Z_U) \\ (\Omega_{UK} + \Omega_{UU}) \cdot (A + (b+e) \cdot C) &= (2b+e) \cdot (\Omega_{UK} \cdot Z_K + \Omega_{UU} \cdot Z_U)\end{aligned}$$

which we may write as

$$\begin{aligned}(2b+e) \cdot \Omega \cdot \begin{bmatrix} Z_K \\ Z_U \end{bmatrix} &= \Omega \cdot \begin{bmatrix} 1 \\ 1 \end{bmatrix} \cdot (A + (b + e \cdot C) \\ \begin{bmatrix} Z_K \\ Z_U \end{bmatrix} &= \begin{bmatrix} 1 \\ 1 \end{bmatrix} \cdot \frac{A + (b+e) \cdot C}{2b+e}\end{aligned} \tag{34}$$

(34) implies that the producers carge the merged shops and the independent shops the same price and that the price level is unaffected by the merger:

$$Z_K = Z_U = Z = \frac{1}{2b + d \cdot m \cdot (m-1)} \cdot A + \frac{b + d \cdot m \cdot (m-1)}{2b + d \cdot m \cdot (m-1)} \cdot C \tag{35}$$

References

[1] Buchanan, J. M., The Theory of Monopolistic Quantity Discounts. *The Review of Economic Studies*, Vol. 20:3, pp. 199-208.

[2] Dobson, P. W. et al (2001), Buyer Power and its Impact on Competition in the Food Retail Distribution Sector of the European Union. *Journal of Industry, Competition and Trade*, 1:3, pp. 247-281.

[3] Fog, Bjarke (1994), *Pricing Theory in Theory and Practice*. Handelshøjskolens Forlag.

[4] Fornell, C. and W. T. Robinson (1983), Industrial Organization and Consumer Satisfaction/Dissatisfaction. *Journal of Consumer Research*, Vol. 6 pp 1-26.

[5] Gilligan, T. W.(1986), The Competitive Effects of Retail Price Maintenance. *The RANDJournal of Economics*. Vol 17:4.

[6] Hovenkamp, Herbert J. (2009), *Analyzing Horizontal Mergers: Unilateral Effects in Product-Differentiated Markets*. University of Iowa Legal Studies Research Paper, No. 09-12.

[7] Inderst, R. and C. Wey (2007), Buyer Power and Supplier Incentives. *European Economic Review.* Vol 51, pp 647-667.

[8] Konkurrencestyrelsen (2007), *CVC's overtagelse af Matas og en række Matasbutikker*. www.ks.dk.

[9] Lustgarten, S. H.(1975), The Impact of Buyer Concentation in Manufacturing Industries. *The Review of Economics and Statistics.* Vol. 57:2, pp 125-132.

[10] Mazzarotto, Nicola (2004), *Retail Mergers and Buyer Power*. CCR Working Paper CCR 04-3.University of East Anglia.

[11] Rosenthal, M.-B. et al (2003), Demand Effects of Recent Changes in Prescription Drug Promotion. *Forum for Health Economics and Policy.* Vol. 6, pp. 1-26.

[12] Snyder, C. M. (1996), A Dynamic Theory of Countervailing Power. *The RAND Journal of Economics.* Vol. 4, pp. 747-769.

[13] Tesler, L. G., (1964), Advertising and Competition. *Journal of Political Economy*. Vol 72, pp. 537-562.

[14] Weng, Z. K. (1995), Channel Coordination and Quantity Discounts. *Management Science*. Vol. 41:9, pp. 1509-1522.

[15] Werden, Gregrory J. and Froeb, Luke M. (2006): Unilateral Competition Effects of Horizontal Mergers. In Paolo Buccirossi, ed., *Handbook of Antitrust Economics*. MIT Press.

In: Economics of Competition
Editors: G. Leismuller and E. Schimpf
ISBN: 978-1-62257-416-2

Chapter 6

WHERE DOES COMPETITION AMONG IRRATIONAL AGENTS LEAD THE MARKET?

Guo Ying Luo*
DeGroote School of Business, McMaster University,
Hamilton, Ontario, Canada

Abstract

The equilibrium notions are derived based on the optimal behavior of rational agents. For example, the notion of perfect competition has been long established based on the presumption of firms maximizing their profits in the process of making their decisions with respect to whether they should enter a market, how much output to produce after they enter the market and when to exit the market. However, with irrational agents in the market instead of rational ones, where does the market competition take the market in the short run or long run? What types of agents would survive in the long run? This chapter intends to review the research results in this part of the literature and point out the future research directions.

1. Introduction

Traditionally, price theory is used to predict the outcome of market competition among firms. The presumption of price theory is that firms are fully rational in

*E-mail address: luogy@mcmaster.ca, Tel: (905)525-9140 ext 23983, Address: Department of Finance and Business Economics, DeGroote School of Business, McMaster University, 1280 Main Street West, Hamilton, Ontario, Canada, L8S 4M4.

every decision they make. So the equilibrium price is established on the basis of optimal behavior of firms. However, firms' rationality of maximizing their profits have been criticized from different angles. Some suggest that firms should pursue other managerial objectives instead of their profits. For example, Baumol (1967) suggests that firms should maximize sales revenue. Williamson (1963) suggests that firms maximize managers' utilities. Cyert and March (1963) suggest that when a firm faces conflicting objectives, it should proceed sequentially to satisfy one objective at a time before considering the fulfillment of others. Also, the organizational complexity of a firm and a business environment of continual dynamic uncertainty presents difficulty for firms to pursue their profits. Simon (1976, 1992) presents his argument that decision makers are often restricted by their forecasting capabilities and limited computational capacity, hence, it is not impossible for firms to accurately maximize their profits or any other objectives.

Now, the question is where the competition take the market if firms are irrational in their decision making process. Penrose (1952), Alchian (1950) and Enke (1951) use Darwinian idea of natural selection to describe the market competition and to predict the market aggregate outcome. As Penrose [11, p.812] points out, "no matter what man's motives are, the outcome is determined not by the individual participants but by an environment beyond their control. Natural selection is substituted for purposive profit-maximizing behavior just as in biology natural selection replaced the concept of special creation of species." Also, as Penrose [11, p.810] paraphrases Alchian [1], "to survive, firms must make profits. Hence positive profits can be treated as the criterion of natural selection—the firms that make profits are selected or 'adopted' by the environment, others are rejected and disappear. This holds whether firms consciously try to make profits or not; even if the actions of firms were completely random and determined only by chance, the firms surviving, i.e., adopted by the environment, would be those that happened to act appropriately and thus made profits. Hence, 'individual motivation and foresight, while sufficient are not necessary,'(Alchian [1950, p.217])." In summary, these early thoughts try to validate profit maximization hypothesis by applying natural selection to market competition. Furthermore, Enke (1951) argues that only the "as if" profit maximizing firms can survive and the resulting market aggregate outcome can be predicted in a way as if firms are maximizing their profits. Enke say, " in the long run, however, if firms are in active competition with one another rather than constituting a number of isolated monopolies, natural selection will tend to permit the survival of only those firms that either through good luck or great skill have managed, almost or completely, to optimize their position and earn the normal profits necessary for survival. In these instances the economist can make aggregate predictions as if each and every firm knew how to secure maximum long-run profits."

Similarly, in financial markets, investors are not able to maximize their utilities and form rational expectation. Investors' behavior can be quite irrational when they submit their bid and ask. Can market efficiency be achieved in the long run when investors are irrational? Friedman's conjecture (1953) suggests that informed traders will gradually take money away from uninformed traders; Informed traders will eventually dominate the market and drive the market price to the fundamental value.

The paper will focus on discussing articles where the rational aggregate market outcome can be generated through natural selection.

The remainder of the paper consists of three sections. Next section discusses articles addressing competition among irrational firms. Articles examining competition among irrational investors in financial markets are discussed in section 3. Final concluding remarks are presented in the conclusion section.

2. Competition Among Irrational Firms

Starting with Winter (1967, 1976), the literature has been trying to analytically validate the profit maximization hypothesis and its predictions on aggregate market behavior although none of their models addresses the resulting aggregate market outcome.

Blume and Easley (2002) construct a general equilibrium model to examine whether the market favors profit-maximizing firms over non-profit maximizing firms. They prove that profit maximizers survive in any steady state of the retained earnings dynamic. However, the long-run behavior of the economy is not consistent with equilibrium models based on the profit-maximization hypothesis.

Luo (1995) builds an evolutionary model where firms enter the market sequentially over time. In this model, firms are completely irrational in their decision making process. That is, firms enter the market regardless of the existence of the profits, exit the market if they use up all their wealth and their outputs are randomly determined upon their entry. Assuming that firms produce homogenous product and the market demand for the product is downward slopping. Luo

(1995) proves analytically that the long-run market outcome is perfectly competitive equilibrium where the surviving firms are those who act as if they are maximizing their profits. To see how the model works, the following presents a detailed analysis of Luo (1995). Consider a dynamic model of a market where firms produce a homogenous good. The market demand for the good is downward sloping. Firms enter the market sequentially over time. For simplicity, only one firm is assumed to enter the market. Note that the results of the model does not depend on the assumption of the number of firms entering the market each period. As long as the number of firms entering the market is finite, the results of the paper hold. When a firm enters the market, the firm pays a fixed amount of entry fee. The entry fee is paid only once by each firm upon its entry. Each firm's output is randomly determined upon its entry. Once its output level is determined, the firm will continue to produce that quantity of the output in all future periods as long as the firm stays in the market. The average variable cost for each firm occurs every period. All firms have the same average variable cost function which is convex with the minimum efficient scale being the profit maximizing output. A firm's profit is defined as the difference between the output price and average total cost multiplying its quantity of output. A firm's wealth at the end of a period is defined as accumulated profits up to the end of that period. If a firm's wealth is negative, this firm exits the market otherwise, this firm will continue to produce the good at the predetermined level.

This market process very much resembles the one for the derivation of perfect competition described in the standard textbook except firms' rationality in the decision making process is removed. In the derivation of perfect competition in the standard textbook, with firms' perfect rationality on their decision making process, firms will continue to enter the market as long as there are positive profits for them in the market and will leave the market if the profits for them are becoming negative. This process goes on until the profit in the market is driven to be zero. At that point, all the remaining firms produce at minimum efficient scale and the perfectly competitive equilibrium is achieved. In Luo (1995), firms enter the market regardless of the existence of profit opportunities, exit the market when their wealth becomes negative and their output is randomly determined upon entry and fixed thereafter. This type of modeling strategy removes firms' rationality in their decision making process. It is the market process itself instead of individual's rationality that determines the long-run survivors and its resulting aggregate market outcome. Specifically, Luo (1995) proves analytically that as the firms get infinitesimally small relative to the market, as the entry cost gets sufficiently small and as time gets sufficiently large, the market converges in probability to a perfectly competitive equilibrium where all the surviving firms are those that happen to produce at the minimum efficient scale and no potential entrants can make positive profits by entry.

Luo (2009) further examines a similar (to Luo (1995)) market process where firms produce similar but differentiated products. In addition, the textbook standard assumptions regarding firms' cost function and demand function are used. That is, firms have symmetric demand functions and identical cost function. Assuming that firms are totally irrational in their decision of entering or exiting the market and their decisions of determining their production levels, with firms entering the market sequentially over times, Luo (2009) proves that the monopolistically competitive equilibrium evolves in the long run where only the firms that happen to produce at the profit maximizing output (or the "as if" profit maximizers) survive. Luo (2011) generalizes the assumptions of Luo (2009) to allow firms to have its own cost functions and demand functions. In this setting, Luo (2011) derives additional results where the long-run surviving firms are those who happen to produce at profit-maximizing outputs and who possess the most efficient technologies and face the most favorable market conditions along with the eventual occurrence of monopolistically competitive equilibrium. Luo (1995, 2009 and 2011) provides analytical support to the conjectures of early economists (e.g., Penrose, Alchian and Enke). In particular, they have modified and supported the classic argument for the derivation of perfect competition and monopolistic competition when firms are irrational in their decision making process.

Luo (1995, 2009 and 2011) presents evolutionary models of market competition with total irrational firms. The economic natural selection in the market favors the survival of the firms who act as if they were maximizing their profits. The long-run aggregate market outcome is rational despite of irrational market participants.

There are some other articles in the literature focusing on investigating in a variety of context the profit-maximization hypothesis without examining the resulting aggregate market outcome. For example, Winter (1964, 1971) sets up a model of retained earning dynamics. He finds that the retained earning of profit maximizing firms grows the fastest and eventually those firms will dominate the market while non-profit maximizing firms will lose money and drain their retained earnings, hence exit the market. Nelson and Winter (1982) constructed a partial equilibrium model where the prices are fixed and all firms have access to the same technology. In this model, they prove that only the "as if" profit maximizing firms are selected in the long-run steady state by the investment dynamic which is based on retained earnings.

Schaffer (1989) comes up with a model of "spiteful behavior" where non-profit maximizing firms can harm its profit-maximizing competitors more than itself by deviating from profit maximizing behavior. This is because firms always possess market power. Hence, the firm is more likely to survive than its profit maximizing competitors. Dutta and Radner (1999) present a dynamic model where an entrepreneur can raise funds for a risky enterprise on a competitive capital market. They find that firms' decision rules which maximize the long-run survival probability are not those which maximize expected profits. In addition, they shows that profit-maximizing firms will not survive in the long run even with the allowance of a finite number of new entrants each period. Beker (2004) shows that if the financial markets are dynamically incomplete and the technology is stochastic, the entrepreneurs operating efficient technologies can be driven out of a competitive market by entrepreneurs operating inefficient technologies.

Comparing Luo (1995, 2009 and 2011) with the other articles mentioned above, the key difference in driving the results of Luo (1995, 2009 and 2011) is that firms in Luo (1995, 2009 and 2011) in the long run have no market power to influence the market price due to the increased competition caused by continuous entry of firms. Whereas firms in other models mentioned above always have market power to influence the market price due to lack of continuous entry of firms.

The next section will discuss where the competition among irrational investors takes the financial markets.

3. Competition Among Irrational Investors

In financial markets, investors have different predictions or beliefs about the future value of the assets. Traders' predictions can be rationally generated from maximizing their utilities or they can be just a matter of behavioral traits observed in the markets, which have no rational basis. If investors in the financial markets are utility maximizers with rational expectation, then informational efficiency can be achieved in the Bayesian Rational Expectation Equilibrium framework (see Grossman (1976, 1978), Radner (1979), Hellwig (1980) and Bray (1981)). However, investors' abilities to maximize their utilities and to form rational expectation about the asset price are very limited. In other words, investors are irrational. Can competition among irrational investors lead a financial market to a rational aggregate outcome (namely, informational efficiency)?

Friedman (1953) conjecture provides a positive answer to that question. That is, natural selection will favor the survival of informed traders who will in turn drive the market to informational efficiency.

Luo (1998) applies the evolutionary idea of natural selection to examine this conjecture and provides analytical support to this conjecture. Specifically, Luo (1998) formulates an evolutionary model of a commodity futures market where the spot price is predetermined each period but unknown to all market participants. Traders are characterized with predetermined probabilities of overpredicting, underpredicting and predicting correctly the spot price. Here, traders' behavior is not coming from maximizing their utilities. Traders' predictions are generated from their predetermined probabilities of predictions about the spot price. These predictions are the bid or ask in the futures market. The futures price is the market clearing price in the futures market. Assuming that each period with a positive probability, the entering trader have a higher probability of predicting correctly the spot price than their predecessors, Luo (1998) proves analytically that with probability one, the futures price converges to the spot price. In the limit, no trader has the market power to influence the futures price. This is due to the fact that in the long run, each individual traders' wealth is infinitesimally small relative to the market wealth. Here, the futures market constantly redistributes wealth among traders. Traders with more wealth will have more influence on the futures price. However, traders with higher probability of predicting the spot price correctly will eventually get selected while others disappear. The informational efficiency arrives as a long-run aggregate market outcome.

Luo (2001) adds a random shock to the commodity futures market of Luo (1998). Again, assuming that with a positive probability in each period, the entering trader has a higher probability of predicting correctly the spot price than their predecessors, Luo (2001) proves that the informational efficiency result depends on the volatility of the random shock in the futures market. In other words, the interval containing the fundamental value, where the futures price eventually lies, is influenced by the underlying volatility generated from the spot market. Hence, the accuracy of the information for which the market can eventually select, depends on the volatility generated from the random shock in the spot market. The more volatile the spot market, the more noisy is the information that gets selected for. As a result, the futures market move further away from informational efficiency. Luo (2003) examines one-sided buyer's auction market in the evolutionary model similar to Luo (1998). Luo (2003) also obtains informational efficiency result provided that each buyer's initial wealth is sufficiently small relative to the market supply.

The key assumption of Luo (1998, 2001 and 2003) in deriving the result of informational efficiency is that with a positive probability each period, the entering trader has a higher probability of predicting correctly the spot price than all previously entered traders. Hence, it is the informed traders who drive the market to informational efficiency. This is exactly as predicted by Friedman's conjecture.

Luo (2012) examines if there is any other reason for the futures market to converge to informational efficiency besides the dominance of informed traders. Hence, Luo (2012) restricts the entry of informed traders by setting the probability of predicting correctly the spot price to be a low number. Luo (2012) also obtains informational efficient results as long as in each period, with a positive probability, entering traders are more conservative than their predecessors. Conservative traders are those who correctly predict the spot price with a positive probability, and more importantly, who in their mistakes err on the side of caution, and rarely overpredict the spot price as buyers, and underpredict the spot price as sellers. The results of Luo (2012) also suggest that no individual trader has market power to influence the futures price in the long run. This is because each individual trader's wealth is infinitesmally small relative to the market wealth. Note that in Luo (2012), more than one type of irrational traders could survive in the long run. This is in sharp contrast with all of other models in the literature where only one type of irrational trader could survive in the long run.

In summary, informed traders in the models of Luo (1998, 2001 and 2003) eventually get selected in the long run and the resulting long-run aggregate market outcome is informationally efficient. And furthermore, no trader has market power to influence the market price in the long run since the wealth of each individual trader is infinitesimally small relative to the market wealth. All the results in Luo (1998, 2001 and 2003) provide analytical support to Friedman's conjecture. However, the results of Luo (2012) do not rely on the entry of informed traders but on the entry of conservative traders. This is a bit surprising since this is not what Friedman thought years ago.

There are other related literature examining whether the market favors the survival of rational agents over irrational agents, however, that group of articles do not examine the resulting aggregate market outcome (e.g., De Long (1991), Palomino (1996), Blume and Easley (1992), Sciubba (2005), Benos (1998), Kyle and Wang (1997), Hirshleifer and Luo (2001), Fischer and Verrecchia (1999), and Kogan, Leonid, Stephen Ross, Jiang Wang, and Ark Westerfield, (2004)). This paper will discuss a few of those articles just for the purpose of comparison.

Sandroni (2000) examines whether the market would select for agents with accurate predictions in a general equilibrium framework with Lucas tree. With the assumption of the intertemporal discount factors being the same for all agents, Sandroni (2000) proves that agents with accurate predictions get selected for eventually and the covergence to rational expectation occurs as agents with less accurate predictions die out. Blume and Easley (2006) further examine this market selection story in a general equilibrium framework. They conclude that the market favors the survival of agents with correct beliefs in the complete market setting regardless of the asset structure (assuming that the intertemporal discount factors are the same for all agents). But the conclusion is not true in the incomplete market. They construct examples to show that the survival of agents with correctly beliefs depends on asset's payoff functions.

Concluding Remarks

Overall, whether the competition among irrational agents lead the market to the rational aggregate market outcome depends on the market structure, market mechanism and irrational agents' behavior. Some articles have presented some market processes in which firms behave totally irrational but the markets are efficient in the long run. Other articles have described how the competition in futures markets can promote efficient aggregate market outcome despite of irrational market participants.

There is a still a lot more work that can be done in terms of identifying market mechanisms that promote market efficiency either through natural selection or through the market structure itself.

References

[1] Alchian, A., (1950) Uncertainty, Evolution and Economic Theory, *Journal of Political Economy,* 58, 211-222.

[2] W.J. Baumol, "*Business Behavior, Value, and Growth,*" rev. ed. Harcourt, Brace and World, New York, 1967.

[3] Beker, Pablo, (2004), "Are Inefficient Entrepreneurs Driven Out Of The Market?", *Journal of Economic Theory*, 114, 329-344.

[4] Benos, Alexandros, (1998), "Aggressiveness and Survival Of Overconfident Traders", *Journal of Financial Markets*, 1, 353-383.

[5] Blume, Lawrence, and David Easley, (1992), "Evolution and Market Behavior", *Journal of Economic Theory,* 58, 9-40.

[6] Blume, Lawrence, and David Easley, (2002), "Optimality and Natural Selection in Markets", *Journal of Economic Theory,* 107, 95-135.

[7] Blume, Lawrence, and David Easley, (2006), "If you're so smart, why aren't you rich? Belief selection in complete and incomplete markets", *Econometrica*.

[8] Bray, M., 1981, "Futures Trading, Rational Expectations, and the Efficient Markets Hypothesis", *Econometrica* 49, 575-596.

[9] R.M. Cyert and J.G. March, "*A Behavioral Theory of the Firm,*" Prentice-Hall, Inc., Englewood Cliffs, N.J., 1963.

[10] De Long, Bradford, Andrei Shleifer, Lawrence Summers, and Robert Waldman, (1991), "The Survival of Noise Traders In Financial Markets", *Journal of Business,* 64, 1-19.

[11] Dutta, P. and R. Radner, (1999) Profit Maximization and the Market Selection Hypothesis, *Review of Economic Studies*, 66, 769-798.

[12] Enke, S., (1951) On Maximizing Profits: A Distinction Between Chamberlin and Robinson, *American Economic Review*, 41, 566-578.

[13] Fischer, P. E. and R. E. Verrecchia. 1999. "Public Information and Heuristic Trade," *Journal of Accounting and Economics*, 27(1): 89-124.

[14] Friedman, Milton, *Essays in Positive Economics*, University of Chicago Press, Chicago, 1953.

[15] Grossman, S.J., 1976, "On the Efficiency of Competitive Stock Markets where Traders Have Diverse Information", *Journal of Finance* 31, 573-585.

[16] Grossman, S.J., 1978, "Further Results On the Informational Efficiency of Competitive Stock Markets", *Journal of Economic Theory* 18, 81-101.

[17] Hellwig, M.F., 1980, "*On the Aggregation of Information in Competitive Markets*", Journal of Economic Theory 22, 477-498.

[18] Hirshleifer, David and Guo Ying Luo, (2001), "On The Survival Of Overconfident Traders In A Competitive Securities Market", *Journal of Financial Markets,* 4, 73-84.

[19] Kogan, Leonid, Stephen Ross, Jiang Wang, and Ark Westerfield, (2004), "The Price Impact and Survival of Irrational Traders", *Journal of Finance,* forthcoming.

[20] Kyle, Albert, and Albert Wang, (1997), "Speculation Duopoly With Agreement To Disagree: Can Overconfidence Survive The Market Test?", *Journal of Finance,* 52, 2073-2090.

[21] Luo, Guo Ying, (1995), "Evolution and Market Competition", *Journal of Economic Theory,* 67, 223-250.

[22] Luo, Guo Ying, (1998), "Market Efficiency and Natural Selection in a Commodity Futures Market", *Review of Financial Studies,* 11 (3), 647-674.

[23] Luo, Guo Ying, (2001), "Natural Selection and Market Efficiency in a Futures Market with Random Shocks, *Journal of Futures Markets,* 21(6), 489-516.

[24] Luo, Guo Ying, (2003), "Evolution, Efficiency and Noise Traders in a One-Sided Auction Market", *Journal of Financial Markets*, 6, 163-197.

[25] Luo, Guo Ying, (2009), "Irrationality and Monopolistic Competition: An Evolutionary Approach", *European Economic Review,* 53(5), 512-526.

[26] Luo, Guo Ying, (2011), "*Natural Selection, Irrationality and Monopolistic Competition*", working paper.

[27] Luo, Guo Ying, (2012), "*Conservative Traders, Natural Selection and Market Efficiency*", working paper.

[28] Nelson, R., and S. Winter (1982), *An Evolutionary Theory of Economic Change*. Harvard University Press, Cambridge, MA.

[29] Penrose, E. T., (1952), "Biological analogies in the theory of the firm", *Amer. Econ. Rev.* 42, 804-819.

[30] Palmino, F. 1996, " Noise Trading in Small Markets, " *Journal of Finance,* 51 (4): 1537-1550.

[31] Radner, R., 1979, "Rational Expectations Equilibrium: Generic Existence and the Information Revealed by Prices", *Econometrica* 47, 655-678.

[32] Sandroni, Alvaro, (2000), "Do Markets Favor Agents Able To Make Accurate Predictions?", *Econometrica*, 68, 1303-1342.

[33] Sciubba, Emanuela, (2004), "Asymmetric information and survival in financial markets", *Economic Theory, forthcoming*.

[34] H. Simon, From Substantive to Procedural Rationality, in "*Method and Appraisal in Economics*" (S.J. Latsis, Ed.), Cambridge University Press, Cambridge, 1976.

[35] H. Simon, M. Egidi, R. Marris and R. Viale, "*Economics, Bounded Rationality and the Cognitive Revolution*," Edward Elgar Publishing Limited, Aldershot, 1992.

[36] O.E. Williamson, Managerial discretion and business behavior, *Amer. Econ. Rev*. 53, (1963), 1032-1057.

[37] Winter, S. (1964), "Economic Natural Selection and the Theory of the Firm," *Yale Economic Essays*, 4, 225-272.

[38] Winter, S., (1971), "Satisficing, Selection and the Innovating Remnant," *Quarterly Journal of Economics*, 85, 237-261.

In: Economics of Competition
Editors: G. Leismuller and E. Schimpf
ISBN: 978-1-62257-416-2

Chapter 7

HETEROGENOUS COMPETITION IN A DIFFERENTIATED DUOPOLY WITH BEHAVIORAL UNCERTAINTY

Akio Matsumoto[a,*] ***and Ferenc Szidarovszky***[b,†]
[a]Department of Economics, Chuo University
742-1, Higashinakano, Hachioji, Tokyo, Japan
[b]Department of Systems and Industrial Engineering
University of Arizona, Tucson, AZ, US

Abstract

This study examines how uncertainty about rival firm's behavior affects the equilibrium and its dynamics under heterogenous competition. A differentiated mixed duopoly is considered in which one firm sets a quantity and the other firm charges a price. It is demonstrated that behavioral uncertainty stabilizes the unstable dynamic process in comparison to behavioral certainty and generates Pareto-improvement in the sense that the firms can earn larger profits.

Keywords: heterogenous strategy, asymmetric product differentiation, behavioral uncertainty, mixed duopoly

*E-mail address: akiom@tamacc.chuo-u.ac.jp
†E-mail address: szidar@sie.arizona.edu

1. Introduction

We study a mixed duopoly model with incomplete or partial information in which one firm adjusts its quantity and the other firm its price but each firm lacks knowledge of the rival firm's strategic behavior (i.e., quantity or price strategy). The mixed duopoly is an intermediate model between a pure Cournot duopoly and a pure Bertrand model, which was first considered by Bylka and Komar (1976) and then extended in various directions. Using a symmetric differentiated duopoly proposed by Dixit (1979), Singh and Vives (1984) showed, among others, that the quantity-adjusting strategy is more (less) profitable than the price-adjusting strategy if the goods are substitutes (complements). Recently Matsumoto and Szidarovszky (2008) constructed a n-firm differentiated mixed oligopoly model with $n > 2$ showing that their result is sensitive to the duopoly assumption. Szidarovszky and Molnár (1992) proved the equivalence of the equilibrium to the non-linear complementarity problem and also proved the existence and uniqueness of the Nash equilibrium in a general N-firm model. These, only to name a few, are static studies. Matsumoto and Onozaki (2005) and Yousefi and Szidarovszky (2005) modeled the dynamic process of mixed duopolies with nonlinear demands and showed the birth of complicated fluctuations.

In this paper we return to the duopoly model and assume uncertainty about the type of strategic variable chosen by the rival firm. We call a situation in which each firm has complete information about the behavior of the rival firm and the market demand *fully-informed* and the one in which each firm has incomplete information about the behavior of the rival firms but complete information about the market demand *partially-informed.* In the recent literature it has been demonstrated that various phenomena may occur as a result of the lack of information about the market demand. Bischi *et al.* (2004) construct a Cournot duopoly in which Nash equilibrium is unique under perfect information and find the emergence of self-confirming steady state and present a situation in which global bifurcation of basin of attraction occurs when firms choose their actions based on a misspecified market demand. Bischi *et al.* (2007) examine a quantity adjustment process of a nonlinear duopoly model and show its stability under incomplete information about the market demand, despite the fact that it can generate complicated dynamics under complete information when the nonlinearities become stronger. In the existing literature, however, very little has been done with respect to the effects caused by the behavioral uncertainty on the equilibrium of the mixed duopoly and its dynamic process.

The main purpose of this study is to shed lights on these unknown effects. In particular, we demonstrate three main results:

1) Incomplete information is chosen endogenously in the presence of exogenous uncertainty about the rival's behavior.

2) Incomplete information stabilizes the market which is unstable under full information.

3) Incomplete information makes Parete-improvement by increasing the profits of both firms.

The remainder of the paper is organized as follows. In Section 2, we present our mixed duopoly model. In the first half of Section 3, we analyze the optimal behavior of the firms with full information in which the behavioral strategy of the firms is common knowledge. Then, in the second half, we reexamine this model with partial information in which the behavioral strategy of the rival firm is unknown. In Section 4, we compare the two types of duopoly equilibria with full information and with partial information. In Section 5, we construct discrete dynamic models in the fully-informed and in the partially informed cases and then show the main conclusions mentioned just above. Section 6 concludes the paper.

2. Cournot–Bertrand Competitions

2.1. Mixed Duopoly Model

There are two firms in a market in which firm i produces good x_i with a constant unit production cost c_i for $i = 1,2$. The inverse demand function of firm i is

$$P_i = \alpha_i - \beta_i x_i - \gamma_i x_j, \tag{1}$$

where $\alpha_i > 0$ and $\beta_i > 0$.[1] By introducing notation

$$p_i = \frac{P_i}{\beta_i}, \quad A_i = \frac{\alpha_i}{\beta_i} \text{ and } \theta_i = \frac{\gamma_i}{\beta_i},$$

[1]It is shown in Singh and Vives (1984) that this linear structure of inverse demand is obtained by maximizing the quadratic and strictly concave utility function

$$U_i(x_1,x_2) = \alpha_1 x_1 + \alpha_2 x_2 - \frac{1}{2}(\beta_1 x_1^2 + 2\gamma_i x_1 x_2 + \beta_2 x_2^2) - \sum_{i=1}^{2} P_i x_i.$$

we obtain the simplified inverse demand functions,

$$p_i = A_i - x_i - \theta_i x_j. \tag{2}$$

Here A_i denotes the reservation price to be attained when demand is zero and is assumed to satisfy the following conditions:

Assumption 1. (a) $A_1 = A_2 = A$; (b) $A > \max(c_1, c_2)$.

Assumption 1(a) is imposed on only for analytical simplicity and Assumption 1(b) is imposed to guarantee interior optimum in maximizing profits of the firms.

The parameter θ_i in (2) denotes the degree of product differentiation. It is the ratio of γ_i over β_i where β_i indicates the direct effect on price p_i caused by a change in x_i and γ_i shows the indirect effect caused by a change in x_j. If $\theta_i = 1$, then both effects are the same and hence the inverse demand functions for $i = 1,2$ become identical, which imply demands for homogeneous goods. If $\theta_i = 0$, then there is no indirect effect. Thus the two goods are independent and the duopoly market is divided into two monopoly markets. A positive or negative θ_i implies that the two goods are substitutes or complements. In this study we confine our analysis to the case in which goods are substitutes and the direct effect dominates the indirect effect.[2] To this end, we make the following assumption:

Assumption 2. $0 < \theta_i < 1$.

Solving (2) with $i = 1,2$ for x_1 and x_2 yields the direct demand of firm i,

$$x_i = \frac{1}{1-\theta_1\theta_2}\left\{(1-\theta_i)A - p_i + \theta_i p_j\right\}. \tag{3}$$

Each firm is either quantity-adjusting or price-adjusting and maximizes its profit by taking its rival's behavior as given. In particular, firm i maximizes its profit

$$\pi_i = (p_i - c_i)x_i \tag{4}$$

[2]Changing the sign of θ_i from positive to negative, we can go from substitutes to complements. Yousefi and Szidarovszky(2005) exhibits emergence of complex dynamics in a nonlinear differentiated duopoly when the indirect effect dominates the direct effect.

subject to either (2) if it is quantity adjusting or (3) if price-adjusting. With two firms and two strategies, there are four possible types of duopoly competition according to the strategy selection of the firms. In this study, we focus on *heterogeneous competition* in which different firms take different strategies: in *Cournot–Bertrand* (*CB*) competition, firm 1 is quantity-adjusting, and firm 2 is price-adjusting and in *Bertrand–Cournot* (*BC*) competition, firm 1 is price-adjusting and firm 2 is quantity-adjusting.[3]

Since Bertrand–Cournot competition is dual to Cournot–Bertrand competition, we restrict our study only to the optimal behavior of firms in *CB* competition. As a benchmark, we start with the case with full information and then proceed to the case of partial information. The optimal values of outputs, prices and profits of the firms under full information are obtained in Section 2.2 and those under partial information will be derived in Section 2.3.

2.2. Full Information Case

Under full information, firm 1 knows that its rival is price-adjusting, sets its quantity x_1, taking its rival's strategic variable p_2 as given. Setting $i = 1$ and substituting (2) into (4) and then substituting x_2 from the solution of (2) give the profit of firm 1 in terms of x_1 and p_2:

$$\pi_1 = \big((1-\theta_1)A - (1-\theta_1\theta_2)x_1 + \theta_1 p_2 - c_1\big)x_1. \tag{5}$$

Firm 2 also knows that firm 1 is quantity-adjusting, charges its price p_2 by taking its rival's strategic variable x_1 as given. Solving (2) with $i = 2$ for x_2 and then substituting it into (4) give the profit of firm 2 in terms of x_1 and p_2:

$$\pi_2 = (p_2 - c_2)(A - \theta_2 x_1 - p_2). \tag{6}$$

Assuming interior optimum and solving the first-order conditions for profit maximization of π_i yields the following forms of the best reply functions:

$$R_1^{CB}(p_2) = \frac{\theta_1}{2(1-\theta_1\theta_2)}p_2 + \frac{(1-\theta_1)A - c_1}{2(1-\theta_1\theta_2)} \tag{7}$$

and

$$R_2^{CB}(x_1) = -\frac{\theta_2}{2}x_1 + \frac{A + c_2}{2}. \tag{8}$$

[3]The remaining two types are Cournot–Cournot competition in which the two firms are quantity-adjusting and Bertrant–Bertrand competition in which both firms are price adjusting.

The superscript "*CB*" attached to functions and variables indicates that they are given in a *CB* competition.

An intersection of these best reply functions is a solution of the simultaneous equations, $x_1 = R_1^{CB}(p_2)$ and $p_2 = R_2^{CB}(x_1)$. In the (p_2, x_1) plane, the $x_1 = R_1^{CB}(p_2)$ curve is positive-sloping and the $p_2 = R_2^{CB}(x_1)$ curve is negative-sloping. Since both curves are linear, there is a unique solution. We call the solution a *CB* equilibrium. The outputs at the equilibrium are

$$x_1^{CB} = \frac{2(A-c_1)-\theta_1(A-c_2)}{4-3\theta_1\theta_2} \tag{9}$$

and

$$x_2^{CB} = \frac{(2-\theta_1\theta_2)(A-c_2)-\theta_2(A-c_1)}{4-3\theta_1\theta_2}. \tag{10}$$

The corresponding equilibrium prices are

$$p_1^{CB} = \frac{-(2-\theta_1\theta_2)(A-c_1)-\theta_1(1-\theta_1\theta_2)(A-c_2)+(4-3\theta_1\theta_2)A}{4-3\theta_1\theta_2} \tag{11}$$

and

$$p_2^{CB} = \frac{-\theta_2(A-c_1)-2(1-\theta_1\theta_2)(A-c_2)+(4-3\theta_1\theta_2)A}{4-3\theta_1\theta_2}. \tag{12}$$

Note that both are positive due to Assumption 2.[4]

Substituting the *CB* outputs and prices into the profit functions presents the *CB* equilibrium profits:

$$\pi_1^{CB} = (1-\theta_1\theta_2)\left(x_1^{CB}\right)^2 \tag{13}$$

and

$$\pi_2^{CB} = \left(x_2^{CB}\right)^2, \tag{14}$$

showing that both profits are positive at the *CB* equilibrium.

[4]The numerators of (11) and (12) are rewritten, respectively, as

$$c_1(2-\theta_1\theta_2)+c_2\theta_1(1-\theta_1\theta_2)+A(2-\theta_1)(1-\theta_1\theta_2)>0$$

and

$$c_1\theta_2+2c_2(1-\theta_1\theta_2)+A(2-\theta_2(1+\theta_1))>0.$$

Before proceeding further, we introduce an alternative expression of the cost ratio,

$$c = \frac{A - c_2}{A - c_1},$$

which is positive by Assumption 1(b). Solving this definition for c_2 gives

$$c_2 = cc_1 + (1 - c)A$$

implying that $c_2 = c_1$ if $c = 1$, $c_2 > c_1$ if $c < 1$ and $c_2 < c_1$ if $c > 1$. Clearly c is closely related to the cost ratio. From (9) and (10), the nonnegativity conditions for the *CB* outputs are given as

$$\frac{\theta_2}{2 - \theta_1\theta_2} \le c \le \frac{2}{\theta_1}. \tag{15}$$

If the marginal cost, c_1, of firm 1 is large enough to make the cost ratio exceed the threshold value $2/\theta_1$, then firm 1 chooses zero-production or exits the market to avoid negative profit. By the same token, if the marginal cost, c_2, of firm 2 is large enough to make the cost ratio smaller than the threshold value $\theta_2/(2 - \theta_1\theta_2)$, then firm 2 chooses zero-production or exists the market. In either case, duopoly competition turns into monopoly. Although it seems to be interesting to consider the birth of monopoly through the duopoly competition with the extreme cost ratio, we confine our analysis to the case when both firms stay in the market.

2.3. Partial Information Case

In *CB* competition with partial information (CB_p competition henceforth), it is assumed that none of the firms have enough information to observe its rival's strategic behavior and therefore each firm determines its best choice, presuming that its rival takes the same strategy. That is, firm 1 thinks that it is in a Cournot competition and firm 2 believes that it is in a Bertrand competition. The profit functions of the firms are therefore defined as follows. Substituting (2) for $i = 1$ into (4) gives the profit of firm in terms of its strategic variable x_1 and the believed strategic variable x_2 of its competitor:

$$\pi_1 = (A - x_1 - \theta_1 x_2 - c_1)x_1.$$

Differentiating π_1 with respect to x_1 gives the first-order condition of profit maximization, which is then solved for x_1 to obtain the best response of firm 1:

$$x_1 = \frac{A - c_1 - \theta_1 x_2}{2}. \tag{16}$$

Firm 2 thinks that it is in a Bertrand competition so its strategic variable is p_2 and believes that its rival sets a price p_1. Substituting (3) for $i = 2$ into (4) gives its profit:

$$\pi_2 = (p_2 - c_2)\frac{(1-\theta_2)A + \theta_2 p_1 - p_2}{1 - \theta_1\theta_2}.$$

Differentiating π_2 with respect to p_2 gives the first-order condition, which is solved for p_2 to derive the best response of firm 2:

$$p_2 = \frac{(1-\theta_2)A + c_2 + \theta_2 p_1}{2}. \tag{17}$$

Due to the partial information, each of expressions (16) and (17) depends on the variable that the rival firm is supposed to choose. To express both best response functions in terms of the decision variables, x_1 and p_2, of the firms, we solve (2) with $i = 2$ for x_2 and (3) with $i = 1$ for p_1 to obtain

$$x_2 = A - \theta_2 x_1 - p_2$$

and

$$p_1 = (1-\theta_1)A - (1-\theta_1\theta_2)x_1 + \theta_1 p_2.$$

Substituting them into (16) and (17) provides the best response functions in terms of the decision variables x_1 and p_2:

$$R_1^{CB_p}(x_1, p_2) \equiv \frac{(1-\theta_1)A - c_1 + \theta_1\theta_2 x_1 + \theta_1 p_2}{2} \tag{18}$$

and

$$R_2^{CB_p}(x_1, p_2) \equiv \frac{(1-\theta_1\theta_2)A + c_2 - \theta_2(1-\theta_1\theta_2)x_1 + \theta_1\theta_2 p_2}{2}. \tag{19}$$

The superscript "CB_p" is attached to functions and variables to indicate that they are given in CB_p competition.

The equilibrium point is defined by a pair (x_1, p_2) such that $x_1 = R_1^{CB_p}(x_1, p_2)$ and $p_2 = R_2^{CB_p}(x_1, p_2)$. Solving these equations simultaneously and using the demand function expressions yield the equilibrium outputs

$$x_1^{CB_p} = \frac{(2-\theta_1\theta_2)(A - c_1) - \theta_1(A - c_2)}{4 - 3\theta_1\theta_2} \tag{20}$$

and

$$x_2^{CB_p} = \frac{2(A-c_2) - \theta_2(A-c_1)}{4-3\theta_1\theta_2}, \tag{21}$$

where the nonnegativity conditions for the outputs are given by

$$\frac{\theta_2}{2} \le c \le \frac{2-\theta_1\theta_2}{\theta_1}. \tag{22}$$

Using (2) with $i = 1$ and $i = 2$, we have the equilibrium prices,

$$p_1^{CB_p} = \frac{-2(1-\theta_1\theta_2)(A-c_1) - \theta_1(A-c_2) + (4-3\theta_1\theta_2)A}{4-3\theta_1\theta_2} \tag{23}$$

and

$$p_2^{CB_p} = \frac{-\theta_2(1-\theta_1\theta_2)(A-c_1) - (2-\theta_2\theta_2)(A-c_2) + (4-3\theta_1\theta_2)A}{4-3\theta_1\theta_2}, \tag{24}$$

both of which are positive. The equilibrium profits are given as

$$\pi_1^{CB_p} = \left(x_1^{CB_p}\right)^2 \tag{25}$$

and

$$\pi_2^{CB_p} = (1-\theta_1\theta_2)\left(x_2^{CB_p}\right)^2. \tag{26}$$

Notice that both profits are positive at the equilibrium.

3. Information Difference

In this section, we compare the equilibrium strategies under full information with those under partial information to show the effects caused by information asymmetry. Based on relations (15) and (22), the parameter region in which equilibrium outputs are non-negative under CB and CB_p competitions is defined by

$$\Theta = \left\{ (\theta_1, \theta_2, c) \mid \frac{\theta_2}{2-\theta_1\theta_2} \le c \le \frac{2-\theta_1\theta_2}{\theta_1} \right\}.$$

We start with firm 1. The output difference is obtained by subtracting (20) from (9),

$$x_1^{CB} - x_1^{CB_p} = \frac{(A-c_1)\theta_1\theta_2}{4-3\theta_1\theta_2} > 0$$

and the price difference by subtracting (23) from (11),

$$p_1^{CB} - p_1^{CB_p} = \frac{(A - c_1)\theta_1\theta_2}{4 - 3\theta_1\theta_2}(c\theta_1 - 1),$$

where $c\theta_1 - 1$ may be positive, negative or even zero.[5] The profit difference is given by subtracting (25) from (13),

$$\pi_1^{CB} - \pi_1^{CB_p} = \left(\sqrt{1-\theta_1\theta_2}x_1^{CB} + x_1^{CB_p}\right)\left(\sqrt{1-\theta_1\theta_2}x_1^{CB} - x_1^{CB_p}\right),$$

in which the first factor is positive and the second factor can be rewritten as

$$\frac{(A - c_1)\left(1 - \sqrt{1-\theta_1\theta_2}\right)\left(\sqrt{1-\theta_1\theta_2} - (1 - c\theta_1)\right)}{4 - 3\theta_1\theta_2}.$$

Since $A - c_1$, $1 - \sqrt{1-\theta_1\theta_2}$ and the denominator are positive,

$$sign\left[\pi_1^{CB} - \pi_1^{CB_p}\right] = sign\left[\sqrt{1-\theta_1\theta_2} - (1 - c\theta_1)\right]. \tag{27}$$

We will next show that $\pi_1^{CB} > \pi_1^{CB_p}$ under economically meaningful conditions.

To determine the sign of the right hand side of (27), we first suppose $c \geq 1$. Then

$$\sqrt{1-\theta_1\theta_2} - (1 - c\theta_1) \geq \sqrt{1-\theta_1\theta_2} - (1 - \theta_1) > 0,$$

where the last inequality is due to relation $\sqrt{1-\theta_1\theta_2} > \sqrt{1-\theta_1} > 1 - \theta_1$ for $0 < \theta_i < 1$. Therefore we have $\pi_1^{CB} > \pi_1^{CB_p}$ for $c \geq 1$. Next suppose that $c < 1$. The $\pi_1^{CB} = \pi_1^{CB_p}$ locus is negative-sloping in θ_1 and defined by

$$\theta_2 = c(2 - c\theta_1),$$

which implies that $\pi_1^{CB} > \pi_1^{CB_p}$ if $\theta_2 < c(2 - c\theta_1)$ and $\pi_1^{CB} < \pi_1^{CB_p}$ if $\theta_2 > c(2 - c\theta_1)$. Returning to the nonnegativity condition of x_2^{CB} and solving it for θ_2 yields that the $x_2^{CB} = 0$ locus is

$$\theta_2 = \frac{2c}{1 + c\theta_1}.$$

[5]If $c \leq 1$ (i.e., firm 1 has a more efficient cost function), then $p_1^{CB} < p_1^{CB_p}$.

Subtracting this equation from the equal-profit locus yields

$$c(2-c\theta_1)-\frac{2c}{1+c\theta_1}=\frac{c^2\theta_1(1-c\theta_1)}{1+c\theta_1}>0,$$

since $0<\theta_1<1$ and $0<c<1$. This shows that the $\pi_1^{CB}=\pi_1^{CB_p}$ locus is located in the region in which $x_2^{CB}<0$. Therefore, $\pi_1^{CB}>\pi_1^{CB_p}$ in the feasible region in which $x_2^{CB}\geq 0$ for $c<1$. Combining this observation with the last result implies that $\pi_1^{CB}>\pi_1^{CB_p}$ in the feasible region in which $x_2^{CB}\geq 0$.

We now compare the equilibrium strategies of firm 2 in *CB* competitions with both full and partial informations. As in the case of firm 1, the output difference and price difference are obtained as follows:

$$x_2^{CB}-x_2^{CB_p}=-\frac{(A-c_2)\theta_1\theta_2}{4-3\theta_1\theta_2}<0$$

and

$$p_2^{CB}-p_2^{CB_p}=\frac{(A-c_1)\theta_1\theta_2}{4-3\theta_1\theta_2}(c-\theta_2),$$

where $c-\theta_2$ may be positive, negative or zero.[6] The profit difference is given by

$$\pi_2^{CB}-\pi_2^{CB_p}=\left(x_2^{CB}+\sqrt{1-\theta_1\theta_2}x_2^{CB_p}\right)\left(x_2^{CB}-\sqrt{1-\theta_1\theta_2}\,x_2^{CB_p}\right),$$

where the first factor is positive and the second factor can be rewritten as

$$\frac{(A-c_2)\left(1-\sqrt{1-\theta_1\theta_2}\right)\left(c(1-\sqrt{1-\theta_1\theta_2})-\theta_2\right)}{4-3\theta_1\theta_2}.$$

Since $A-c_2$, $1-\sqrt{1-\theta_1\theta_2}$ and the denominator are positive,

$$sign\left[\pi_2^{CB}-\pi_2^{CB_p}\right]=sign\left[c(1-\sqrt{1-\theta_1\theta_2})-\theta_2\right]. \tag{28}$$

We can also show that $\pi_2^{CB}<\pi_2^{CB_p}$ under economically meaningful conditions.

[6]If $c>1$ (i.e., firm 2 has a more efficient cost function), then $p_2^{CB}>p_2^{CB_p}$.

To determine the sign of the right hand side of (28), we first suppose that $c \leq 1$. Then

$$c\left(1-\sqrt{1-\theta_1\theta_2}\right)-\theta_2 \leq 1-\theta_2-\sqrt{1-\theta_1\theta_2} < 0,$$

since $\sqrt{1-\theta_1\theta_2} > \sqrt{1-\theta_2} > 1-\theta_2$ for $0 < \theta_i < 1$. Therefore, $\pi_2^{CB} < \pi_2^{CB_p}$ as $c \leq 1$. Next suppose that $c > 1$. The $\pi_2^{CB} = \pi_2^{CB_p}$ locus is negative-sloping in θ_1 and defined by

$$\theta_2 = c(2-c\theta_1),$$

which implies that $\pi_2^{CB} < \pi_2^{CB_p}$ if $\theta_2 < c(2-c\theta_1)$, and $\pi_2^{CB} > \pi_2^{CB_p}$ if $\theta_2 > c(2-c\theta_1)$. Returning to the nonnegativity condition of $x_1^{CB_p}$ and solving it for θ_2 implies that the $x_1^{CB_p} = 0$ locus is

$$\theta_2 = \frac{2-c\theta_1}{\theta_1}.$$

Subtracting it from the equal profit locus yields

$$c(2-c\theta_1) - \frac{2-c\theta_1}{\theta_1} = \frac{(2-c\theta_1)(c\theta_1-1)}{1+c\theta_1} > 0.$$

The last inequality is due to $c\theta_1 - 1 > 0$ which is shown as follows. The $x_1^{CB_p} = 0$ locus crosses the horizontal line $\theta_2 = 1$ at $\theta_1^! = \frac{2}{1+c}$, which implies that the feasible domain of the $x_1^{CB_p} = 0$ locus is the interval $[\theta_1^!, 1)$. For $\theta_1 > \theta_1^!$,

$$1 < \frac{2c}{1+c} < c\theta_1.$$

The direction of the inequality implies that the $\pi_2^{CB} = \pi_2^{CB_p}$ locus is located in the region in which $x_1^{CB_p} < 0$. Therefore, $\pi_2^{CB} < \pi_2^{CB_p}$ in the feasible region in which $x_1^{CB} \geq 0$ for $c > 1$. Combining this observation with the last result implies that $\pi_{12}^{CB} < \pi_2^{CB_p}$ in the feasible region in which $x_1^{CB_p} \geq 0$. We can summarize the above result as follows:

Theorem 1. *In the feasible parameter region in which $x_1^{CB_p} \geq 0$ and $x_2^{CB} \geq 0$, the quantity-adjusting firm earns more profit in the fully informed case than in the partially informed case (i.e., $\pi_1^{CB} > \pi_1^{CB_p}$) while the price-adjusting firm earns more profit in the partially informed case than in the fully informed case (i.e., $\pi_2^{CB} < \pi_2^{CB_p}$).*

In comparing the equilibrium strategies under full information with those under partial information, an interesting phenomenon can be noticed: the equilibrium strategies under partial information are the duals of the equilibrium strategies under full information. Comparing the equilibrium output levels (9) and (10) with (20) and (21), the equilibrium prices (11) and (12) with (23) and (24), and the equilibrium profits (13) and (14) with (25) and (26), we can see that they are identical if we interchange the two firms (i.e., $x_i^{CB} = x_j^{CB_p}$, $p_i^{CB} = p_j^{CB_p}$ and $\pi_i^{CB} = \pi_j^{CB_p}$ for $i, j = 1, 2$ and $i \neq j$). Since the CB$_p$ competition is dual to the BC competition ($\pi_1^{CB_p} = \pi_1^{BC}$ and $\pi_2^{CB_p} = \pi_2^{BC}$), Theorem 1 can be alternatively summarized as $\pi_1^{CB} > \pi_1^{BC}$ and $\pi_2^{CB} < \pi_2^{BC}$, which is the result shown by Singh and Vives (1984). Although the equilibrium values are the same, it does not necessarily imply that the dynamic processes are also identical. We will now turn our attention to the analysis of the dynamic processes.

4. Stability Analysis

In this section, we investigate the stability of the CB equilibrium and that of the CB$_p$ equilibrium. If the firms have naive expectations and the time scale is discrete, then the best reply discrete dynamics under full information is constructed as follows:

$$\begin{cases} x_1(t+1) = \dfrac{\theta_1}{2(1-\theta_1\theta_2)} p_2(t) + \dfrac{(1-\theta_1)A - c_1}{2(1-\theta_1\theta_2)}, \\ \\ p_2(t+1) = -\dfrac{\theta_2}{2} x_1(t) + \dfrac{A+c_2}{2}. \end{cases} \tag{29}$$

This is a two dimensional linear system with coefficient matrix

$$J^{CB} = \begin{pmatrix} 0 & \dfrac{\theta_1}{2(1-\theta_1\theta_2)} \\ \\ -\dfrac{\theta_2}{2} & 0 \end{pmatrix}.$$

The eigenvalues of the associated characteristic equation are

$$\lambda_{1,2} = \pm i \frac{1}{2} \sqrt{\frac{\theta_1\theta_2}{1-\theta_1\theta_2}},$$

which are inside the unit circle if and only if

$$\theta_1\theta_2 < \frac{4}{5}. \tag{30}$$

In addition to this stability condition, we need to take the nonnegativity constraints (15) on the outputs, x_1^{CB} and x_2^{CB}, into account to obtain the proper condition for the stability of the CB equilibrium:

Theorem 2. *In a CB competition with full information, the unique CB equilibrium is feasible and stable if the degrees of the product differentiation, θ_1 and θ_2, and the cost ratio, c, are in the following set:*

$$\Theta^{CB} = \left\{ (\theta_1, \theta_2, c) \mid \ \theta_1\theta_2 < \frac{4}{5}, \ \frac{\theta_2}{2-\theta_1\theta_2} \le c \le \frac{2}{\theta_1} \right\}.$$

We now continue with examining the stability of the CB_p competition. Assuming naive expectations again, the best reply discrete dynamics under partial information is as follows:

$$\begin{cases} x_1(t+1) = \dfrac{\theta_1\theta_2}{2} x_1(t) + \dfrac{\theta_1}{2} p_2(t) + \dfrac{(1-\theta_1)A - c_1}{2}, \\[2ex] p_2(t+1) = -\dfrac{\theta_2(1-\theta_1\theta_2)}{2} x_1(t) + \dfrac{\theta_1\theta_2}{2} p_2(t) + \dfrac{(1-\theta_1\theta_2)A + c_2}{2}. \end{cases} \tag{31}$$

This dynamic system is also two-dimensional and linear with coefficient matrix

$$J^{CB_p} = \begin{pmatrix} \dfrac{\theta_1\theta_2}{2} & \dfrac{\theta_1}{2} \\[2ex] -\dfrac{\theta_2(1-\theta_1\theta_2)}{2} & \dfrac{\theta_1\theta_2}{2} \end{pmatrix}.$$

The characteristic equation is quadratic in λ,

$$\lambda^2 - \theta_1\theta_2\lambda + \frac{\theta_1\theta_2}{4} = 0.$$

It is easy to verify that its eigenvalues are inside the unit circle since the stability conditions of this two dimensional system are satisfied under Assumption 2:

$$1 - \det J^{CB_p} = 1 - \frac{\theta_1\theta_2}{4} > 0$$

and

$$1 \pm trJ^{CB_p} + \det J^{CB_p} = 1 \pm \theta_1\theta_2 + \frac{\theta_1\theta_2}{4} > 0.$$

In addition to these conditions, the outputs $x_1^{CB_p}$ and $x_2^{CB_p}$ are subject to the nonnegativity conditions (22). Hence our second stability result can be summarized as follows:

Theorem 3. *In a CB competition with partial information, the unique CB_p equilibrium is feasible and stable if the degrees θ_1 and θ_2 of the product differentiation and c are in the following set:*

$$\Theta^{CB_p} = \left\{ (\theta_1, \theta_2, c) \mid \frac{\theta_2}{2} \leq c \leq \frac{2 - \theta_1\theta_2}{\theta_1} \right\}.$$

As in Section 3, let Θ denote the region of parameters θ_1, θ_2 and c where the equilibrium outputs are nonnegative in both *CB* and CB_p competitions. It can be divided into two parts by the $\theta_1\theta_2 = 4/5$ locus,

$$\Theta = \Theta_s \cup \Theta_U$$

with

$$\Theta_s = \left\{ (\theta_1, \theta_2, c) \in \Theta \mid \theta_1\theta_2 < \frac{4}{5} \right\} \text{ and } \Theta_U = \left\{ (\theta_1, \theta_2, c) \in \Theta \mid \theta_1\theta_2 \geq \frac{4}{5} \right\}.$$

As Figure 1 shows, the lighter-gray region is Θ_s, the darker-gray region is Θ_U and one or two non-negativity conditions are violated in the white regions.

Comparing these stability conditions with those under partial information, we first notice that less information improves stability since the fully-informed dynamic process is unstable while the partially-informed process is stable in region $(\theta_1, \theta_2, c) \in \Theta_U$. We then notice that collecting information on the rival's strategy by both firms to change the partially informed competition to fully informed competition is advantageous for firm 1 since $\pi_1^{CB} > \pi_1^{CB_p}$ and disadvantageous for firm 2 since $\pi_2^{CB} < \pi_2^{CB_p}$, regardless of whether the CB equilibrium is stable or not.

As a result of profit maximizing behavior of the firms, it may be reasonable to assume that firm 1 will collect information about the behavioral strategy of its rival, make it known to firm 2 as well as fully informs the competitor about its own behavioral strategy in order to change the partially informed oligopoly into

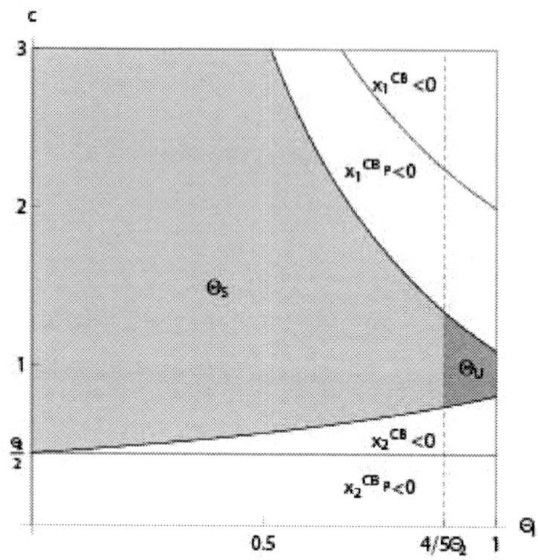

Figure 1. Division of the fesible region by the stability condition.

the fully informed case. However there is no guarantee that firm 2 will believe and trust firm 1 in this message, so the price adjusting firm will continue believing that it is in a partially informed mixed oligopoly. Hence CB competition with asymmetric information endogenously emerges. In this case, firm 1 has the best reply function $R_1^{CB}(p_2)$ and firm 2 has $R_2^{CB_p}(x_1, p_2)$. An intersection of these best reply functions is an equilibrium state under asymmetric information which is denoted by $(x_1^{CB_a}, p_2^{CB_a})$ with

$$x_1^{CB_a} = \frac{(2-\theta_1\theta_2)(A-c_1)-\theta_1(A-c_2)}{(4-\theta_1\theta_2)(1-\theta_1\theta_2)} \tag{32}$$

and

$$p_2^{CB_a} = A - \frac{\theta_2(A-c_1)+2(A-c_2)}{4-\theta_1\theta_2}. \tag{33}$$

Similarly to (29) and (31), the corresponding discrete dynamic system with naive expectations is given by

$$\begin{cases} x_1(t+1) = \dfrac{\theta_1}{2(1-\theta_1\theta_2)}p_2(t) + \dfrac{(1-\theta_1)A-c_1}{2(1-\theta_1\theta_2)} \\[2ex] p_2(t+1) = -\dfrac{\theta_2(1-\theta_1\theta_2)}{2}x_1(t) + \dfrac{\theta_1\theta_2}{2}p_2(t) + \dfrac{(1-\theta_1\theta_2)A+c_2}{2} \end{cases}$$

with coefficient matrix

$$J^{CB_a} = \begin{pmatrix} 0 & \dfrac{\theta_1}{2(1-\theta_1\theta_2)} \\ -\dfrac{\theta_2(1-\theta_1\theta_2)}{2} & \dfrac{\theta_1\theta_2}{2} \end{pmatrix}.$$

The CB$_a$ equilibrium is asymptotically stable, since all stability conditions are satisfied:

$$1 - \det J^{CB_a} > 0 \text{ and } 1 \pm trJ^{CB_a} + \det J^{CB_a} > 0$$

where

$$\det J^{CB_a} = \frac{\theta_1\theta_2}{4} \text{ and } trJ^{CB_a} = \frac{\theta_1\theta_2}{2}.$$

We summarize this result as follows:

Theorem 4. *In a CB competition with asymmetric information, the unique CB$_a$ equilibrium is feasible and stable if* $(\theta_1, \theta_2, c) \in \Theta$.

This stability result implies that even if firm 1 has full information and firm 2 has only partial information, they can still arrive at the CB_a equilibrium. Since this holds for $(\theta_1, \theta_2, c) \in \Theta_U$, we find again that less information stabilizes the otherwise unstable full information equilibrium.

The equilibrium values of the other variables are

$$p_1^{CB_a} = \frac{-2(A-c_1) - \theta_1(A-c_2) + (4-\theta_1\theta_2)A}{4-\theta_1\theta_2} \tag{34}$$

and

$$x_2^{CB_a} = \frac{-\theta_2(A-c_1) + (2-\theta_1\theta_2)(A-c_2)}{(4-\theta_1\theta_2)(1-\theta_1\theta_2)}. \tag{35}$$

We can also obtain the equilibrium profits of the two firms under asymmetric information:

$$\pi_1^{CB_a} = \frac{1}{1-\theta_1\theta_2}(x_1^{CB_a})^2 \tag{36}$$

and

$$\pi_2^{CB_a} = \frac{1}{1-\theta_1\theta_2}(x_2^{CB_a})^2. \tag{37}$$

Then we have the following results concerning profit comparisons:

Theorem 5. *Equilibrium profits obtained at the CB_a equilibrium are larger than the profits obtained at any other equilibria:*

$$\pi_1^{CB_a} > \pi_1^{CB} \text{ and } \pi_2^{CB_a} > \pi_2^{CB_p}.$$

Proof. Using (9), (10), (32) and (35), it can be shown that

$$x_1^{CB} - x_1^{CB_a} = -\frac{\theta_1^2\theta_2}{(4-3\theta_1\theta_2)(4-\theta_1\theta_2)(1-\theta_1\theta_2)} x_2^{CB} \leq 0$$

and

$$x_2^{CB_p} - x_2^{CB_a} = -\frac{\theta_1^2\theta_2}{(4-3\theta_1\theta_2)(4-\theta_1\theta_2)(1-\theta_1\theta_2)} x_1^{CB_p} \leq 0,$$

where the inequalities are due to the non-negativity conditions of x_2^{CB} and $x_1^{CB_p}$. Based on Assumption 2, the following profit ratios are greater than unity

$$\frac{\pi_1^{CB_a}}{\pi_1^{CB}} = \frac{1}{(1-\theta_1\theta_2)}\left(\frac{x_1^{CB_p}}{x_1^{CB}}\right)^2 > 1 \text{ and } \frac{\pi_2^{CB_a}}{\pi_2^{CB_p}} = \frac{1}{(1-\theta_1\theta_2)}\left(\frac{x_2^{CB_a}}{x_2^{CB_p}}\right)^2 > 1.$$

Since $\pi_1^{CB} > \pi_1^{CB_p}$ and $\pi_2^{CB_p} > \pi_2^{CB}$ have been already shown in Theorem 1, the proof is complete. ■

Concluding Remarks

In this study we constructed mixed duopoly models with full information and with partial information in which one firm is quantity-adjusting and the other is price-adjusting but each firm has uncertainty about the rival firm's behavioral strategy. If the competition starts with partial information, firm 1 finds it profitable to collect information on the rival's strategic behavior (i.e., quantity-adjusting or price-adjusting), tells this knowledge to the competitor as well as informs it about its own strategic behavior to change the partially informed oligopoly to a fully informed competition. If firm 2 does not trust its rival in this message, then it may continue believing that the oligopoly is still partially informed, so a CB competition with asymmetric information emerges.

Our main conclusions are summarized as follows:

1) CB competition with asymmetric information is a natural consequence in the presence of exogenous uncertainty about the rival firm's behavior.

2) Asymmetric information stabilizes the market in the sense that the CB_a equilibrium is stable even if $(\theta_1, \theta_2, c) \in \Theta_U$.

3) Asymmetric information makes Pareto-improvement since both firms can make larger profits at the CB_a equilibrium than at any other equilibria.

Acknowledgment

The authors highly appreciate financial supports from the Japan Society for the Promotion of Science (Grant-in-Aid Scientific Research (C) 21530172), Chuo University (Joint Research Grant 0981) and the Japan Economic Research Foundation. They also want to acknowledge the encouragement and support from Kei Matsumoto for the research leading to this paper. Part of this paper was done when the first author visited the Department of Systems and Industrial Engineering of the University of Arizona. He appreciated its hospitality over his stay. The usual disclaimer applies.

References

Bischi G.-I., Naimzada A., Sbragia L. (2007) Oligopoly games with local monopolistic approximation. *Journal of Economic Behavior and Organization*, 62, 371–388.

Bischi G.-I., Chiarella C., Kopel M. (2004) The long run outcomes and global dynamics of a duopoly game with misspecified demand functions. *International Game Theory Review*, 6, 343–379.

Bylka S., Komar J. (1976) Cournot–Bertrand mixed oligopolies. In M. Beckman and H. P. Künize eds., *Warsaw Fall Seminars in Mathematical Economics* 1975 (Lecture Notes in Economics and Mathematical Systems 133), Springer-Verlag, 22–33.

Dixit A. (1979) A model of duopoly suggesting a theory of entry barriers. *Bell Journal of Economics*, 10, 20–32.

Matsumoto A., Szidarovszky F. (2010) *Price and quantity competition in differentiated oligopoly revisited.* DP#183 of Economic Research Institute, Chuo University, 1–28.

Matsumoto A., Onozaki T. (2005) Heterogenous strategies in nonlinear duopoly with product differentiation. *Pure Mathematics and Applications*, 16, 443–466.

Singh N., Vives X. (1984) Price and quantity competition in a differentiated duopoly. *Rand Journal of Economics*, 15, 546–554.

Szidarovszky F., Molnár S. (1992) Bertrand, cournot and mixed oligopolies. *Keio Economic Studies*, 26, 1–8.

Yousefi S., Szidarovszky F. (2005) Once more on price and quantity competition in differentiated duopolies: a simulation study. *Pure Mathematics and Applications*, 16, 515–531.

INDEX

D

E

J

L

M

N

O

P

R

S

T

U

V

W

Y